THE POETRY TRIALS

POETS OF THE FUTURE

Edited by Emily Wilson

First published in Great Britain in 2016 by:

 Young**Writers**

Remus House
Coltsfoot Drive
Peterborough
PE2 9BF
Telephone: 01733 890066
Website: www.youngwriters.co.uk

FOREWORD

Welcome, Reader!

For Young Writers' latest competition, *The Poetry Trials*, we gave secondary school students nationwide the challenge of writing a poem. They were given the option of choosing a restrictive poetic technique, or to choose any poetic style of their choice. They rose to the challenge magnificently, with young writers up and down the country displaying their poetic flair.

We chose poems for publication based on style, expression, imagination and technical skill. The result is this entertaining collection full of diverse and imaginative poetry, which is also a delightful keepsake to look back on in years to come.

Here at Young Writers our aim is to encourage creativity in the next generation and to inspire a love of the written word, so it's great to get such an amazing response, with some absolutely fantastic poems. It made choosing the winners extremely difficult, so well done to *Patrick Thurlow* who has been chosen as the best in this book. Their poem will go into a shortlist from which the top 5 poets will be selected to compete for the ultimate Poetry Trials prize.

I'd like to congratulate all the young poets in
The Poetry Trials - Poets Of The Future - I hope this
inspires them to continue with their creative writing.

Jenni Bannister

Editorial Manager

CONTENTS

King Edward VI School, Stratford-Upon-Avon

King's College Alicante, Alicante

Lewis Girls' Comprehensive School, Hengoed

North Coast Integrated College, Coleraine

Ramsey Grammar School, Isle Of Man

THE POEMS

LET ME

Let me go
and I'll float above this rotten place.
Everything is uglier up close
but high in the sky
you can see every side.
It may be wrong
to wish you away,
but can't you see
I need to be alone?

Let me go
and I'll run from your life.
I see you with her,
but it still hurts.
You anchor me down,
I sink and drown.
Why do you care?
I'm in despair.

Let me fall
and I'll fall for him.
You saw us kiss
but you seemed to miss
when we made stories in the fire,
shaping our future.
Do you have room
for one more broken soul?

Let me hang
and now your head hits the floor.
Two lovers, lay side by side
no one ever understood
how much their love was to die for.

Nikki Aisha Hamon (15)

OVERLOOKED

As the child wakes, so does her room,
It is not dramatic; it doesn't come to life with a *boom*,
So, as she turns off her alarm,
The clock waves its hands, content and calm.
She walks off with a brisk pace,
Leaving a frown on the poor clock's face,
Next, as she sits down at the table,
Her chair rises to the challenge, strong and stable.
Its legs never fail and he doesn't get tired,
It is this reason he can't be fired.
She picks up her bag and pulls out her book,
Stealthily, it gives her an angry look,
For this book's spine has been bent and torn,
From day one it was thumbed and worn.
Next, she puts on her clothes and her shoes,
But they were feeling a case of the blues.
They were covered in mud from yesterday,
After they went to the park to play.
Next, she sat in her chair for a lesson,
With the whiteboard being written on by a person.
But once the board discovered its story
It was wiped away with glory.
These items may look ordinary to you,
But don't forget that they have feelings too.

Eleanor Foster (13)
Alcester Grammar School, Alcester

WAR AND CONFLICT

W e will obliterate
A nyone and
R epulse and

A ny acts of brutal
N egativity
D o not fool us with your spiteful ideas

C onduct yourself with honour
O nly magnanimous soldiers stay
N obel and
F ree
L iberate those
I n
C onflict, stay
T ruthful.

Jarrad Baines (12)
Avon Park School, Rugby

THINGS THAT GO BUMP IN THE NIGHT

Spooky, scary skeleton
assassinations imminent to happen,
any second,
Dead people rise from their graves
munching and maliciously killing for
the fun of it.
Assassins rising up, killing more
and more, until they're all dead!
On the ground, no guards to stop
the reign of terror on Halloween night.
The next day, it will be a ghost town
until the next Halloween night!

Danny Dunk (11)
Avon Park School, Rugby

THINGS THAT GO BUMP IN THE NIGHT

I want to murder all the poems in the world,
I want to make it so that they are swirled
in a tornado of death,
Where they take their final breath!
I hate that it rhymes when it doesn't rhyme,
It wastes my time.
I don't know, but writing this makes me
think of heavy metal,
like Slayer.
Maybe they'll hear me and answer my prayers
and get rid of poetry forever.

Ella Harris (12)
Avon Park School, Rugby

WHAT GOES BUMP IN THE NIGHT

When wolves howl and spiders crawl,
noises running on the walls.
Yet, there's one sound that rules them all,
which leaves the question, what goes bump in
the night?
Is it a world of fright,
some ceremony in the night,
or something having a bite,
metal clanging terrifying them all?
One thing's for certain, lie in fours,
lock your doors and don't forget to ask . . .
'What goes bump in the night?'

Benjamin Fletcher (11)
Avon Park School, Rugby

COMRADESHIP

C ompany
O n one's own - never
M emorable
R elationships
A uspicious and
D edicated
E ngaging in
S olidarity
H elping
I nspire
P ositivity.

Ellis Storer (12)
Avon Park School, Rugby

THINGS THAT GO BUMP IN THE NIGHT

In the wild there are wolves howling and spiders crawling,
Lions pouncing and danger lurking and hawks stalking
Clouds spreading and rain falling
I wouldn't go into the wild at night
Because I'm sure dangerous
Animals are waiting
To give you the fright of your life.

Dylan Tilley (11)
Avon Park School, Rugby

JUDGEMENT

Cruel, sunken eyes shackled into place
Protruding from every deadly face
Reaching into your soul like a beggar on the street
Bombarding you with their thoughts, dragging you down to your feet.

Each one takes to the stand and whispers words of pain
Biting, chewing, gnawing at your emotions until you're driven insane
From acidic tongue and disease-ridden mind,
It's the most heavenly soul in which a devil you shall find.

The gavel strikes the block, like thunder on the ground
Your heart cracks like glass when it hears the reckoning sound
The jury rises high with invisible black wings
And sneers like a crow, wreaking havoc, it sings.

The tidal wave in your brain drowns the smiles you once beamed
The nightmares assassinate the future of which you've always
dreamed
The roses in your garden all fall and wilt away
The petals fly hopelessly into the gloomy distance, having lost their
sunny day.

You've learnt dark secrets about yourself, you know they don't exist
But even with your tears and determined roars, the serpents still
persist
You turn the tables, fight back with anger and draw a dagger to their
throat
But the words have spread like wildfire, the invaders have crossed
the moat.

The jury shuffle off to make their choice in silence,
But the destruction of your name is loud
You sink to your knees with no powers left, you're still alive but you
feel bereft
The people reappear, stood like Grim Reapers waiting to kill
Their fists are clenched tightly and their breath leaves a deadly chill.

But even with a guilty verdict, you've won the case at heart
Regardless of the colours you were painted with, you remain a work of art
You gulp and sigh at the moody stares but the light is waiting within
You walk away like a hero undaunted, having not committed a single sin.

James Connolly (15)
Aylesford School, Warwick

EVERYTHING COMES TO AN END

Have you ever been so much in love,
where there's only that one person
just you and them?
Being treated as if you're royalty,
having small surprises,
to show a token of their love,
taking time as it goes,
whilst making each and every moment worthy,
living in that precious moment
that will once become a memory,
wanting it to last . . . forever?
But forever isn't as long as you think.
Forever is a seven-letter word,
but so is goodbye.
After having every heartfelt moment
with your other half,
it all of a sudden becomes a heartbreak.
Have you ever had your heart broken?
Literally the feeling of -
the pain
the smashing
the shatter
and worst of all the break.
Everything comes to an end,
even in death.

Gabriella Maloney (14)
Aylesford School, Warwick

LET'S ABOLISH SLAVERY ONCE MORE

My brother, oh, my brother!
I need work, I need money, someone help!
Once was light and free!
Now...
It's dark, it's cramped, I can't breathe!
Someone help!
No one can hear my screams, I can't scream!
Beaten, tortured, abused, raped, I can't escape!
I can't do anything but the job!
Someone help!
Another day passes, still in Hell, will I ever see Heaven?
Heaven is just a dream!
I hope Heaven's a better place!
Someone help!
Food, hunger, thirst, I just need something!
My body is against me!
I can't think anymore, who am I?
Someone help!
Sweating, working, labour day by day!
Tired, drained, lifeless, day by day!
No freedom for the rest of my days!
Someone help!
When will this slavery end?
Will it end?
All I wanted was a job, security, money, help!
It's far from what reality gave!
No rights, no soul, no life!
Someone help!
Anyone, please help!
Let's abolish slavery once more!

Ann Donaldson (16)
Aylesford School, Warwick

BULLY

You should know that bullying hurts,
It starts with one word, the one word you blurt.
Ugly, unpopular and a waste of space, these are the words they could hear,
But did you know that people felt the fear?

Day by day, you torment me,
It may take some time, but I need to be free,
I will ask for one true friend,
But you make me want it to end.

When enough is enough
And I'm sick of playing tough,
I want them to know I can make it through,
You may not know, but this is true.

You can see, all I wanted was a friend,
Someone to stand by me when the bullying comes again,
Now I am free,
The insults barely affect me.

The bully is never wanted, unless wanted to leave,
The people you have bullied have no need to grieve,
Your work here is done, not that it should have begun,
Now you can see what you have done.

Bullying gave you that power, that they refused to give,
Now you can't help but wonder, 'What if?'
What if they weren't that strong?
What was it like all along?

Alice Goodman (14)
Aylesford School, Warwick

FEMINISM

Let us give some constructive criticism
About something they call feminism
Women have always been oppressed
But now, they wish to be the best.
It's not about equality or equal rights with them
A lot of them just want the downfall of men.
Granted, not all think this way
As a lot of men still get their say
But some feminists don't think like this
They only dream of equality and bliss
All men and women with the same rules
None of us even being treated like fools.
Yet, somewhere there are women who think men
Are so much weaker than them
We get more jail time for things we do
Even when women do it too.
Women can be emotional and no one would judge
Men, however, have to be resolute and keep hold of that grudge.
A lot of women still believe in the genders living together
Holding on as equals, supported by a tether
But still we get these feminists who claim men aren't as good
Still, we are equal, as we should.

Jamie Sayer (14)
Aylesford School, Warwick

A LESSON TO LEARN

Titanic, unsinkable!
And nobody wants war,
All so believable
When Germany is knocking on Poland's door.

Possible labour troubles,
Fiddlesticks!
All living in their reality-proof bubbles,
Missing out on all of life's kicks.

No lesson learned,
No respect earned,
No responsibility accepted,
What can be expected?

A future of shame,
Only yourself to blame,
What good is money
When your future isn't very sunny?

But, if you learn in time…
And you accept the consequences of your actions,
You'll learn a lesson that will last a lifetime,
Then your future brightens.

Jamie Clay (14)
Aylesford School, Warwick

CONFLICT

(Lipogram - A)

Conflict occurs everywhere, not only with soldiers
It will kick off with only one word or text
The person who tries to begin conflict might just be envious of you
Not everyone will die, but it will still hurt
Conflict might not be punches or pushes, it hurts with words
But if you stop, no one will get hurt
So think before you text or do something.

Corey McVicker (14)
Ballymoney High School, Ballymoney

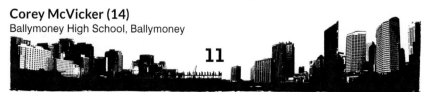

11

THE TEENAGER

One day a lovely girl,
Went into town,
And started to sing,
But everyone covered their ears.

They screamed for her to be quiet,
And she was annoyed,
She took a mood swing,
In the middle of the town.

And was angry,
That no one liked her,
This little girl's singing,
She ranted and raved.

But her time was up,
She went home,
In a mood swing,
That no one could cure.

She went into the kitchen,
And vegetables awaited,
For her tum to eat,
She screamed and shouted.

But no one cared,
She sat down to her
Vegetables that awaited her,
On a plate with mash
And a tub of gravy dip.

This little girl,
That loved to sing,
Just wanted to be noticed,
And to be a normal teenager,
Like all her friends in school.

Emma Edgar (12)
Ballymoney High School, Ballymoney

OVER AS SOON AS IT STARTED

I got the call late that night,
The national team offer,
This massive opportunity had been given to me,
I thought, *I've got to take this.*

The first game against our rivals,
The biggest one of all,
As I sat on the bench,
Watching the minutes tick by,
As shots rocketed by
And tackles flew in,
You could tell, it was a heated rivalry.

Gaffer turned around,
Pointed and smiled,
It was the 60th minute,
My chance had arrived.

I got on the pitch
Pumped up for a game,
The adrenaline was rushing fast.
Players were tiring,
I got the ball and ran,
The defence was shoddy,
I got straight through,
Only the keeper now,
I chipped it over him.

I got it straight from kick-off,
My touch was awful,
The opposition came flying in,
Studs up, two-footed,
Leg breaker, it was all over.

Jude Bolton (12)
Ballymoney High School, Ballymoney

FREE LLAMA!

Look, it's a llama!
That llama's running free!
There goes that llama
As happy as can be.

Out the steel zoo gates,
Jumping through the grass,
People stare at him,
While in their cars they pass.

Running across the road,
Bringing cars to a stop!
Running free is llama
Being chased by a cop!

'Can we adopt that llama?'
Said Timmy from up the lane,
'I will get you that llama
If you stop being a pain.'

They took in the llama,
Calling him John Lee,
But llama was not happy,
So again, he ran free.

Look, it's a llama!
That llama's running free!
There goes that llama
As happy as can be.

Adam Cunningham (12)
Ballymoney High School, Ballymoney

HOMELESS

As I look back on my childhood,
All the bad memories come floating back in like a river,
Battered and abused by my parents,
My life as a child was not a good memory.

After, I could take no more,
I ran away from my abusive home,
Left homeless, out on the filthy street,
With no food to eat.

There were other homeless people on the street,
They gave me some cardboard on which to sleep,
Every day I would beg for money,
Then all the rich people would look down on me.

They looked at me with pity in their eyes,
One of them took me in
And now I'm not homeless.

Oh, how I remember that street,
Damp, dark and homeless
Will be with me for evermore.

Kirsten Moore (13)
Ballymoney High School, Ballymoney

SEA

An opening to a new world
a place that looks dead
also is flowing with life.
Blue all around,
seems like all are barely moving.
In a murky blue, fish flow,
millions and millions all around.
No way a place for a weak person,
a place which is especially deadly,
also, even more full of colour.

Arthur Taggart
Ballymoney High School, Ballymoney

15

OH THE JOYS OF BEING A TEENAGER!

Oh, the joys of being a teenager,
The mood swings and hair fixes,
Checking social media every hour,
Finding out your best friends have been gossiping about you!

Getting angry about the spot in the middle of your forehead,
Then trying to cover it up with make-up,
Describing your parents as a social hand grenade,
Because they are embarrassing.

There can be good things, like finding your first love,
Making new words like 'banter',
Nowadays, it's all about having your eyebrows 'right'
People will judge you on the way they are.

I think the hardest thing about being a teenager
Is your body image,
If you have the right clothes or the in-style ones,
But I guess, that's all part of being a teenager!

Lucy Mitchell (12)
Ballymoney High School, Ballymoney

WINTER

(Lipogram - A)

Winter is Mr Frost's best friend,
The sound of children jumping in the snow,
People worried to drive,
Getting the kids to school;
The kids keep their fingers crossed.
Everywhere you look, snowmen, plus shop discounts.
When you stroll down the drive,
Can only smell lovely chicken dinner.
This is winter.

James Drain (13)
Ballymoney High School, Ballymoney

16

MISS YOU DAD

On the 14th September,
I lost my dad.
He was everything to me,
I remember being outside
Learning to ride my bike
And then him driving me to school.

When he passed away
I thought my world was crumbling around me,
Nothing and nobody was slowing down.

Everyone just got on with their lives.

It's not true when someone says,
'It will get better,'
It never does.
You learn to cope with it,
Time really does heal.
Love you Dad.

Olivia Gillian Martha McCloy (13)
Ballymoney High School, Ballymoney

RED

(Lipogram - T)

Red, like flames burning in open fires
Like sparks off fireworks reaching higher and higher
Love in spring, so fresh and pure
Like poppies in some fields, lying calm
Red, like summer sun shining down
Making us feel happy, so no need for frowns
Red is a happy colour,
Cheerful as well as bringing joy
For everyone around.

Holly Forgrave
Ballymoney High School, Ballymoney

SISTERS

Sisters are the ones you get jealous of
When they get better Christmas presents!
Or when they blame you for something that you didn't do
And your parents believe them all the time.

They are also the ones you get annoyed at
When they pull your hair,
When they punch and slap
Also when they kick!

They're always telling you how much they hate you
And how much they wish you'd never been born!
Whether they are younger or older than you
You will always be family.

I'm glad to have a sister to look out for me
When we argue, they have no idea how much I love them
I've known them my whole life
I hope soon you will truly see how much you mean to me!

Chloe Parkhill (12)
Ballymoney High School, Ballymoney

PINK

(Lipogram - T)

Pink is like a flower's new beginning
in life, or a bowl of fresh raspberries.
A sun, fading, can be similar
as well as a pair of cherry-pink lips.
Pink flows like a pink rose
or a daisy in bloom,
she is bubblegum you chew all day
or your rosy cheeks
when you feel like sugar!

Cailin McMullan
Ballymoney High School, Ballymoney

BALLYMONEY HIGH

B oys running in corridors, pushing people
A nnoying teachers is a plus
L ots of screaming in the playground
L osing our minds in maths class
Y oung students, with tight ties
M obiles hidden under the desk
O verwhelming joy at the end of the day
N obody knows what they're talking about
E veryone would rather be at home
Y elling across the dinner hall

H oping that we didn't get homework tonight
I diots thinking they're smart
G irls thinking they're joining the circus
    with the amount of make-up they put on
H onestly, it's not that bad though.

Joshua Walker
Ballymoney High School, Ballymoney

BALLYMONEY HIGH

B est year ever
A lot of work
L essons that are really fun
L ecture only for the bad people
Y esterday, the day we started school
M usic, the best subject ever
O ther subjects that are good
N ever give up and do your best
E very day makes me happy
Y elling kids down the corridor

H elping people
I ntelligent students
G irls running about the place
H ilarious times we've had here.

Marc William Tweed (12)
Ballymoney High School, Ballymoney

19

IMMIGRANTS TO REFUGEES

Strangers, they keep coming
They are brave but also scared
They are risking their lives to come to paradise
These immigrants are homeless and hungry.

These people are bringing family members
These immigrants are increasing every day
These immigrants are dying, thinking they're escaping.

These immigrants are now called refugees
They're happy as can be to get away
These refugees are jumping into vans dangerously.

Getting sent back to their country
Their worst nightmare for them
These people, now called refugees are needing help
Who will help them?

Lily McMullan (12)
Ballymoney High School, Ballymoney

REVENGE

He hated school,
Everyone treated him like a fool,
They didn't know what he did when he was at home,
Especially when he was alone,
The things they did, didn't help him at all,
Instead of rising he would fall,
They would shove, kick and call him names,
Why would they not let him join their games?

One day, he thought, *why should I care?*
Maybe he could give them a scare,
He hid around the corner, this will be fun,
He screamed loudly and they began to run,
How do you feel when it happens to you,
Especially when you're only new.

Elie Munnis (12)
Ballymoney High School, Ballymoney

20

PARENTS

Parents are the ones who can make you frown,
They annoy you and nag you,
But parents are also the ones who pick you up when you fall down,
I'm sure you know all this too.

Parents are the ones who ground you,
The ones who scold you when you're bad,
But parents are also the ones that care for you
And comfort you when you're sad.

Parents are the ones who won't let you eat sweets,
Because the dentist won't like it,
But parents put food on my plate each week,
I can't deny that one bit.

But even through rough times,
I will love my parents forever.

Beth Wilson (12)
Ballymoney High School, Ballymoney

BALLYMONEY HIGH

B is for boys who won't be quiet in class
A is for A+ grade standards
L is for learning to the best of our ability
L is for laughing all day long
Y is for your achievements
M is for my targets
O is for other subjects
N is for numerous classes
E is for enthusiastic pupils
Y is for yearning to go home at the end of the day

H is for high standard grades
I is for infectious laughter
G is for great achievements
H is for hilarious laughs.

Caitlyn Apperley (12)
Ballymoney High School, Ballymoney

21

MY TWIN BROTHER

My twin brother is a bore
He leaves his shoes all over the floor
His drawers are a mess
Mine are the best

I'm always dressed neatly for school
But he always looks like a fool
I'm great at work
And he is a real jerk

Why do you push me around
And throw me to the ground?
You eat like a pig
Maybe, that's why you're so big

Deep down, you're still my twin brother
And I would never choose another.

Olivia Heaney (12)
Ballymoney High School, Ballymoney

THE LONE WALKERS

They travel by day and by night,
From country to country, these lone immigrants walk.
Battered and bruised from jumping fences,
Avoiding soldiers as hard as they can go.

Stranded, unwanted, homeless and scared,
Worn-out shoes, not a penny to their name,
All for comfort and compassion,
They want to be wanted when they lie awake,
Hail, rain or shine, their hearts still go on.

Refugees we call them, nobody wants them,
'We don't want them,'
'Get out!' people shout, 'we're full!'
Will they ever find peace or a home at that?

Craig Hanna (12)
Ballymoney High School, Ballymoney

GIRAFFE

Zebras are stripy, just like my striped giraffe,
Clumsy and adopted he was
Until he tumbled and tripped and called, 'What a laugh!'
That was the end of my giraffe.

Horrible thing though,
His death was not the real cause,
He had flattened the president,
But the president got back up and said,

'Burn this, it's a riot!
And sue this terrible owner,
In fact, lock him away
And make sure he doesn't see the light of another day.'
That was the end of John McRay.

Jay Steele (12)
Ballymoney High School, Ballymoney

YEAR 8 ACROSTIC POEM

B e on your best behaviour
A lways be on time
L isten to your teachers
L earn new things
Y ou will be looking up to the elders
M ake new friends
O rganisation will get you credits
N ever break the rules
E veryone is welcome
Y ear 8 is the best.

Corey McIntyre (12)
Ballymoney High School, Ballymoney

DISMISS MOVIES

(Lipogram - T)

Space, a place of peace,
You're gliding across endless plains of silence,
Dismiss movies from your mind
Because no one knows for real.

Moons, rocky worlds and sparkling heavenly bodies,
You could never be somewhere more secluded.
If you could keep your life for a few seconds more,
Endless blue and endless purple would consume you.

Dylan Nutt (14)
Ballymoney High School, Ballymoney

CONFLICT

(Lipogram - A)

Conflict, bullets going everywhere.
Running, hiding for your life,
fighting for your country.
Blood dripping from bodies
while bombs drop from the sky.
Soldiers creeping through trenches.
Hunger, terror, tension, stress.
The world is in ruins!

Keelan Clark (13)
Ballymoney High School, Ballymoney

BLACK

(Lipogram - T)

Black is a colour of sorrow
A loved one passing away
Like a crow on a branch
A January evening sky
Black is a funeral dress
A blackboard in school
Like a main road
A pair of school shoes.

Jack Campbell (13)
Ballymoney High School, Ballymoney

LIGHT IS . . .

The definition of a dream,
A dream that will never come true,
The happiness of a family,
The love of a couple,
A resource of emotions,
The friendship between the moon and the sea,
The beauty of a sunset,
The tears of a new mum,
The romance of a candlelit dinner,
The cry of a new baby,
A new life coming into the world,
The fire of a bush camp,
The sea reflecting the moon,
The confidence between a mum and her daughter,
The first smile of a little baby,
Kids playing in the snow,
The eyes of someone who sees an old friend,
The tears of a real person,
The eyes of parents marrying their daughter,
Behind the darkness . . .

Charline Mugnier (12)
College Jacques Monod, Les Pennes-Mirabeau

LIGHT IS . . .

Making us hop,
showing us the way of life,
a source of happiness,
a shimmering sea of shiny stars,
an old mountain where the sun rises,
a place where we feel good,
a fiery kingdom,
a flaming torch in an old castle,
a white, wild horse galloping in a dark night,
a child running in a field of flowers,
an angry dragon breathing fire,
a heaven where dreams come true,
a universe empty of fantasy,
a lonely man searching for a kindred spirit,
he is walking and walking . . .
but can't find it,
his soulmate is the dark, running after him,
they will never be together, but will always be running after
themselves,
without the light, we would be nothing,
because the light is everything.

Eveline Mironov (13)
College Jacques Monod, Les Pennes-Mirabeau

LIGHT IS . . .

A lamp post in the middle of a pitch-black night,
a dream that will never come true,
two persons madly in love,
laughter of children,
happiness in hearts,
the crying of a newborn baby,
a new life coming into the world,
a firework exploding in the night,
the anxiety when it's the first day of school.

Noa Duffau (10)
College Jacques Monod, Les Pennes-Mirabeau

LIGHT IS ...

The warm sunshine,
The love of two people,
The opposite of dark,
Something you want to bring to the world,
The lovely morning sunshine,
The white dog at the beach
And fireflies over the lake,
Happiness in our eyes,
The next world paradise,
What people try to catch,
A gorgeous sunrise you need in your life.

A place where the horrific dark can't be victorious,
The reverse of pain,
The glory,
The delightful butterflies,
Something that makes you happy,

Life is just ...
The eternal ...
    Life.

Antoinette Gomez (13)
College Jacques Monod, Les Pennes-Mirabeau

LIGHT IS ...

Light is yellow fires shooting from the sky to light the world
Light is street lights flashing on a speeding car
Light is motivation to rise
Electric lights flowing through my veins
Light is a text message in the middle of the night
Light is me, playing video games in the night
Light is a reflection on a piece of tape
Light is the feeling of my new shoes in the dark
Light burns my eyes in the morning
Not fair!

Michael Mbodwan (10)
College Jacques Monod, Les Pennes-Mirabeau

27

LIGHT IS ...

Illuminating us at home
Discovery for science
Glowing in the darkness
And horrendous if there is too much
thousands of colours
Heaven or Hell
Incredible
Sensitive
Thinking and talking
Perfectly white
Oil burning
Electric power
The trail to paradise
Romantic in a sunset
Maybe your destiny.

Cedric Roccia (12)
College Jacques Monod, Les Pennes-Mirabeau

LIGHT IS ...

A phoenix in the sky
Sun shining on the sea
Fire on a torch
God's radiant whiteness
An omnipresent object
Yellow particles
A king's crown
A lighthouse
A flashlight in the night
The sparkles in a baby's eye
The path to Heaven
A beautiful dream
Golden ingots
A philosopher's ideas
Maybe the day of tomorrow.

Jonathan Boyer (12)
College Jacques Monod, Les Pennes-Mirabeau

LIGHT IS ...

Light is a feather on paper
Light is essential for life
Light is blinding you by the sun
Light is a shiny boat coming in from the darkness
Light never fades away
Light is the moving sun
Light will not disappear one day
The beautiful day started by light
It's a beautiful voice, saying 'Life!'
Light is a vivid inspiration
Light is the reason to live on Earth.

Light is life.

Victoria De Bank (12)
College Jacques Monod, Les Pennes-Mirabeau

LIGHT IS ...

An explosion of a million stars,
A majestic lion,
A light bulb of hope,
A fiery phoenix,
A door to Heaven,
A spark of true happiness,
A sky where dreams come true,
A magical moon of love,
A sunrise shared by soulmates,
An infinite fire,
A forest of fireflies,
A melting candle.

Emma André (13)
College Jacques Monod, Les Pennes-Mirabeau

LIGHT IS ...

The way to Heaven
the start of each day
like a blooming flower
the beginning of life
a huge, warming fire
a lightning bolt zigzagging at full speed
the moon and the sun
a light bulb appearing over people's heads
a colourful rainbow that fills the sky
a flash that reassures everyone
the joy of Christmas
a force that scares the dark away, guiding us.

Léo Félicés (14)
College Jacques Monod, Les Pennes-Mirabeau

LIGHT IS ...

What comes after night,
What blinds you from darkness,
What's beautiful but dangerous,
Something so close that we can't touch it,
Too big to control,
Flames which don't hurt,
A small thing between others,
The contrast on paper from all the black lines,
So strong that it can die at any moment,
A flash of electricity,
A small thing, but filling all the space,
What blinds a baby from its birth.

Yan Kelleghan
College Jacques Monod, Les Pennes-Mirabeau

LIGHT IS ...

The first discovery
The hope of mankind
New life
Creativity of nature
The last colours
Infallible, immortal, imperial, important
The beginning
What attacked the darkness in that fight for the universe
The first and last thing that was and will be on the Earth
The last things we lost
What the moon, the Earth, the men
all the animals need to exist.

Liam Baron (14)
College Jacques Monod, Les Pennes-Mirabeau

THE LIGHT IS ...

Light is an invisible rainbow
Light is the gift of the sun
Light is the filter of the sky
Light is where the moon is hiding
Light is a shadow compared to Heaven
Light is what gives us a reason to live
Light is an idea born in a head
Light is a diamond's reflection
Light is the enemy of darkness
Light is a secret word that you can only read with a mirror
Light is the path to follow to go to the beyond.

Raphaël Honnet (12)
College Jacques Monod, Les Pennes-Mirabeau

LIGHT IS . . .

A colourful nebula in the deepest, darkest space
A Christmas tree in a dark winter
A knight in shining armour fighting a dark dragon
A vibrant firework on a wonderful summer night
Where everybody goes
A crackling fire near a river
The stairway to Heaven
A snowy peak
A blooming tulip
The photographer's pen
The fuel for many living things.

Emilien De Bank (13)
College Jacques Monod, Les Pennes-Mirabeau

LIGHT IS . . .

The flash of ideas come to my brain
a beautiful sunset at 11pm
an awesome lunar eclipse
a reassurance ghost
a place where dreams live
a best friend
love forever
the evolution of humans
the beginning of a new, exciting day
the powers of a fairy
kisses from a prince to a princess.

Maëlle Chiarello (11)
College Jacques Monod, Les Pennes-Mirabeau

LIGHT IS . . .

Light is untouchable.
Light is one of the deepest colours.
Light is what comes from the biggest planet of our system.
Light is what helps but hurts.
Light is the human beings' reason.
Light is the start and the end of a life.
Light is the angelic side of someone.
Light is the high voltage that helps in dark parts of life.
Light is an everyday used object.
Light is the love in hearts.
Light can't be seen in intricate detail.

Leopold Sarr (12)
College Jacques Monod, Les Pennes-Mirabeau

LIGHT IS . . .

A white dot on a black piece of paper
A lamp post in the night
The screen of a phone
The sun shining in the sky
The flash of a camera at a party
Heaven
An angel coming down the sky
A colossal star shining in the night
The moon glowing in the black sky
Birth
The day.

Maya Fosseux (12)
College Jacques Monod, Les Pennes-Mirabeau

LIGHT IS ...

A giant fire
a group of candles playing a pleasant melody
an incredible source of creativity
a flower growing, but not dying
the beginning of another amazing day
the long way to Heaven
creating rainbows which make us happy
scaring the dark away with authority
Christmas, lots of light bulbs dancing together
warming up the small rabbit during winter.

Adrien Caltagirone (11)
College Jacques Monod, Les Pennes-Mirabeau

LIGHT IS ...

The start of a spring day
A reflection of love in a colourful eye
The birth of a new baby
A beautiful rainbow after a dark sky
Guiding us for our destiny
A lost torch in a black shadow
The stars passing in front of your eyes in space
The beginning of a happy Christmas
A couple of ideas that come out in a kid's imagination
A bolt of lightning that falls because of an angry sky.

Victor Chardonnet (14)
College Jacques Monod, Les Pennes-Mirabeau

LIGHT IS ...

Love in the air
Friends at the door
Feathers falling
Happiness
A daydream
The beautiful moon in the sky
The sun in my heart
Blinding me with her beauty
Liberty
Peace in the world.

Carla Idri (11)
College Jacques Monod, Les Pennes-Mirabeau

LIGHT

The thing which is always there,
The wink of light through the window tonight
Where you go when you are cold,
The spark of electricity in darkness

You are the thing that makes a feather a thing on a bird's flight
When a baby sees for the first time when she comes out of her
mother's womb
Heaven in its brightest
Life as we speak!

Harout Res Albarian (11)
College Jacques Monod, Les Pennes-Mirabeau

LIGHT IS . . .

A white horse running through a black swamp
A flower blooming in a desert fire
on a freezing day for a homeless person
The doorway to Heaven
A rainbow on a cold, rainy day
A light bulb in a pitch-black room
A lightning bolt on a stormy evening.

Youvraj Khatwani (15)
College Jacques Monod, Les Pennes-Mirabeau

CHRISTMAS

Brilliant, fabulous, amazing,
Christmas calls you,
Gifts, food and songs,
Christmas cards too.

Family, carols, midnight mass
And Santa's coming too!

So shout, 'It's Christmas'
Glorify your family
And jump with joy,
A good Christmas Day
Is right in front of you.

Davina Jarwaa (11)
Etone College, Nuneaton

MY MUM

Behind your shadow
I rise and fall
living a life
in which I feel so small

The feelings for you
you might think dumb
blue, upset, confused
down, hurt, numb

Wanted a mum
but you weren't there
to talk about boys
or show that you care

Yes, you did call
every once in a while
but an ocean of weeping
hides behind my smile

Tormented, hidden, torn
I don't like to feel
even after being reborn
my heart still won't heal

I see other girls
giggle with their mums
I go dizzy with swirls
getting hit by the bomb

Where were you Mum?

Keely-Louise Gardner
Etone College, Nuneaton

STRINGS

The strings hang limply from the puppeteer's skilled hands,
Thinking about its next move, I must obey its commands,
I walk around, a silent, unheard scream echoes through the place I
used to call my mind.
The puppeteer grins, for I am forced to stay confined,
Dancing around on broken limbs, a Cheshire cat grin on its lips.

I slowly spiral down into a pit of darkness,
Like a ghost, I fade into the abyss, losing my alertness,
'My little puppet, you must not fade yet, the nightmare has only
begun.'
I am a broken doll, I danced and danced, I spun and spun,
Cold sweat running down my neck, a shiver clinging to my spine.

A shadow follows me everywhere I go, its taunting laugh echoing in
my head,
I turn around and instead, see a long, white thread.
Looking up at the grey sky, it grins down at me, golden eyes taunting
me,
Around and around I spin, as hard as I try, I cannot flee.
Fingers move carefully, like a spider's legs, shadowing my every
move.

One last time, I take a bow in front of the stage,
Choking back a sob, so I must make my last stand,
I use the last shred of willpower I have left,
I shatter the mirror and defy my enemy's hand.
Reality and dreams shatter and fall, gripping a piece of the mirror, I
sever the strings,
No time to think about consequences, no time to think about the cut
that stings,
Through all the fear, I manage a smile before everything around me
shatters.

'My little puppet, freedom can be achieved, but it comes at a price.'
I lie on the cold ground, colour seeping from my cuts, I have rolled the dice,
The puppet lies broken, but on its face a peaceful smile replaces the usual fearful wince.
The puppeteer watches silently and walks away, never to be seen since.
Beware its golden eyes and skilled hands,
For webs are carefully set out to ensnare you
In the world of dreams and nightmares.

Meritxell Castaner Saltos (14)
European School Of Brussels IV, Brussels

ALONE

Ever since I was a little girl
I was left alone and afraid
Until you came to my aid
You treated me like a precious pearl

I was alone with only my nightmares
Until you came to my aid
Although you led me astray
You freed me from all my cares

It was too good to be true
One day you were there
The next, you were just a nightmare
You disappeared into the blue

I start to wonder now
Were you ever real?
I don't even remember how you feel
I still miss you anyhow

Were you just a dream
Within this endless nightmare?
I used to not have a single care
But now it seems it was all just a dream.

Irene Fazio (14)
European School Of Brussels IV, Brussels

39

ROOTED IN PLACE

I once saw a man who

Was stuck in a tree
And stayed rooted in place for fifty years
So after a while we told him to go and see the world

'Do I have to?' he asked. 'I've been
Rooted in place for fifty years.'
'Enough!' we told him. 'Go see the world and find a place to settle.'
And so we offered to help him find his ideal location
My friend asked, 'What kind of place do we need?'
'In the forest, ' I said, 'or in the countryside.'
'No luck in the forest,' the courier said, 'try your luck in 20 years.'
Going back to his house, the baker said, 'He's bolted his door and
won't move.'

The old man's house was hidden away
He indeed refused to get out or walk out of bed
'It must be cruel to move a creature of habits, it
Seems, once you are rooted in place you may not move.'

The old man tried, but he could not move
In this instance he couldn't grasp any material
Many of these objects, his hand passed through
Every object seemed a projection, a cruel immaterial trick.

Anton James Girard-Sequeira (14)
European School Of Brussels IV, Brussels

THE END

It was a beautiful day
Perfect for a walk
The girl ran out of the house
And down the hill.

Across meadows, full of buttercups
And mountains, topped with snow
Until she reached the beach
With golden sand.

The water was calm
And all she could hear was its ripples
Sliding up and down
The silent cove.

Far in the distance
But steadily approaching
Was a bird
As big as the girl

The bird swooped down
Gently lifting the girl into the air
Taking her back to reality.

Polly Barber (14)
European School Of Brussels IV, Brussels

A NIGHTMARE

My breath is short, my head is turning,
my legs are heavy, my thoughts are churning.

Out loud I try to cry, I try to scream,
but no sound comes out from deep within.

At a black painting, in cold sweat, I stare,
falling into a dark abyss in scare.

My clock starts ringing and I open my eyes,
it was just a dream, what a great surprise!

Leandro Buzzino (15)
European School Of Brussels IV, Brussels

THE DARK KNIGHT

I was awoken in the black of night
by the heavy footsteps of an armoured knight
a man in heavy black armour came and said
that by the end of the night he would have me dead

I jumped out of bed and flew down the stairs
but as it turns out he was already there
the knight in black armour opened his mouth and said
that by the end of the night he would have my head

I ran around the house, into the room with Mother's blouse
in the seconds of silence, I stayed quiet as a mouse
the knight in black armour burst the door and said
that by the end of the night he would see me dead

I ran from the room and slid under a chair
and of course, he came and found me there
then his sword came down to split my head
and then he said I was finally dead.

Daniel Navas (14)
European School Of Brussels IV, Brussels

DAYDREAM BELIEVER

The brightest of lights
Guiding me through the nights
Showing me around my mirage
Disguised in camouflage

I walk through the ocean of sand
With no one to hold my hand
And with what is left
My only companion is my shadow of death

As the distance separating me from the oasis
My mouth, my heart, my soul fall into the abyss
No more illusions, at last I am free
I am liberated from my agony.

Maxime Pierre Allen (15)
European School Of Brussels IV, Brussels

42

ONE'S DREAM FOR ONE'S FAMILY

I and my family are from dreams awoken,
We are almost completely broken!
We run frantically from the Jihad's roar
To the Occident's peaceful core.

As we hold our hopes and dreams close, we dash,
The tyranny spreads through the lands like an agonising rash.
We seek refuge,
In our hopes and dreams which remain huge.

I dream of my children learned and learned they shall be,
From war-scarred they won't be,
However, no matter how much I am persistent
The tyranny is the more resistant.

All I can do now is let my kin dream,
While I fight to make it seem
We live without torment
And we live without having to lament.

Conor Mac Donnchadha (14)
European School Of Brussels IV, Brussels

DREAMS AND NIGHTMARES

Dreams are made up of good and bad thoughts,
Some you remember when morning dawns,
Not everyone dreams,
Some of us don't,
Why that happens
No one knows.

Nightmares come when in a deep sleep,
Scary as Hell, they can give you the creeps,
When nightmares are bad and you jump out of bed,
You fall on the floor and you bang your head.
You turn on the light and gather your thoughts,
Wondering, what on earth, could have made you so fraught.

Alan O'Reilly (15)
European School Of Brussels IV, Brussels

43

BEING AN ADOLESCENT

Being an adolescent
Is not easy
Your parents being incessant
About getting you off the TV
And when you want to do something with your friends
Your parents will always say no
'Well son, it depends,
Will you clean the whole house before you go?'
Another problem is the amount of schoolwork
That we are expected to always do
The stress making us berserk
So we rush through
Like our childhood
As fast as a stream
We say that our adolescence is not good
But compared to adulthood, it is all just a dream.

Oisín O'Byrne (14)
European School Of Brussels IV, Brussels

BLACK SHEEP

Was it not a simple dream?
All there was, was a black sheep,
Is it not a dream when I'm not asleep?
Only thing I could do was scream.

The night was too dark,
To tell if it was only a black sheep.
Was I still asleep?
Was it just a sheep in a park?

Robert Rittweger (14)
European School Of Brussels IV, Brussels

NIGHTMARES

The pills, the people
The harsh light of day
All putting my fears to sleep
The ocean that is my pillow
The tears and hopes that drown me.

We are human, therefore we ache
We lie, and talk about the
Future, making our guesses
Stuck in elusive reality
Our own respective
Nightmare.

Sorcha Murphy (15)
European School Of Brussels IV, Brussels

I'M NOT WHO YOU REALLY THINK I AM

I'm not who you really think I am
I'm not perfect
I'm not grand
I make mistakes, more than anyone else I know
So please, don't look for a perfect glow
I am vulnerable, I laugh, I cry
And yes, I can be shy
You should take me off your pedestal and bring me down to Earth
And stop trying to determine my worth
Yes, I was lost, I was angry, I was confused
But that doesn't mean I should be accused
So listen to me when I say, we are together here
Because none of this is meant to last forever.

Samsara Manet-Bhaskar (14)
European School Of Brussels IV, Brussels

IMMERSED IN A DREAM WORLD

This distorted world, a mirror of my own,
is nothing but a riddle to my senses.
The wind, the flowers, all seem so real
that I slowly let down my defences.
My hand's reaching out, groping for the known,
through roving mists and fleeting shadows.
I walk on the canvas of my subconscious alone
and with every step, reality becomes a stranger.

Chloé Ten Brink (15)
European School Of Brussels IV, Brussels

AFTERLIFE

The afterlife, an unknown area
We can visit our knowns there, but never go.
You might get malaria
and not even know.
You might get shot,
the afterlife is where you'll go.
Someone, left dead in the snow
you know where they'll go, the afterlife, bro!

Ross Paltiel (14)
European School Of Brussels IV, Brussels

LIGHT

White but colourful,
Raving rays,
Cognoscenti,
Life it pays.

Shone where happiness,
Lost where fight,
Declined through abyss,
When stole is right.

Found by sparkle
Of eyes it seems,
So controversial,
But familiar gleam.

Red, orange, yellow,
Green, yet blue,
Indigo, violet,
Slowly burns through.

Pearl as beauty,
Weightless white blades,
Rapider than nimble,
Straight colonnades.

Blazing fury,
Incandescent fear,
When the end of light's story
Is drawing near.

Failed in death,
Used in sight,
The crowning breath
Of all its might.

Effulgent of sight,
Resplendent with might,
Lambent and boisterous,
Scintillating effulgence.

Patrick Thurlow (13)
King Edward VI School, Stratford-Upon-Avon

METEOR

The bright soaring,
Elegant roaring,
Vivid light in the depth of the night,
Hunting its prey,
Mother Earth,
Illuminous,
Majestic death,
Comforting fear,
Flickering the last rays of hope,
Radiant,
Fiery,
Gliding,
Riding,
Across the jet-black sky,
Homing in,
Preparing to destroy.

Mass destruction everywhere,
Turn, twist, jive, jump,
Try and find the culprit,
Mass destruction everywhere,
No matter where you go,
Chaos,
Flicking, licking flames,
Engulfing everything in its path,
Surrounded,
A now ugly ogre,
Burning in agony,
Yet delight,
Its mission complete,
Yet once a soaring beauty,
A diamond jewel trailing bright light in the night,
Taking advantage of its glory and sight
Now prevailed its power and might.

James Edward Rowe (12)
King Edward VI School, Stratford-Upon-Avon

DARKNESS

Light is no more,
Turned off by a switch,
Turned off by God,
Turned off by loss of life,
Replaced by me.

Their fire extinguished,
Their bodies useless, lifeless,
Their souls,
Their minds,
Drifting away,
Replaced by me.

Their families grieving,
Their houses empty, abandoned,
Their friends,
Their relations,
Grieving,
Replaced by me.

I am the absence of light,
Of life,
I am sadness,
Death,
I am heavy nothingness,
Black and unforgiving.

I will last till the end of time,
Outlasting,
Outliving,
I am everything and nothing.

I
Am
Darkness.

Romain Philippe Tissut (13)
King Edward VI School, Stratford-Upon-Avon

FIREWORK

Austere darkness; nothing there
Heavy blackness; lingering
Unrelenting nothingness
Shadow of a long dead light.

Suddenly shooting
Spiralling up
Faster and faster
A streak of bright light.

Screaming banshee
Shooting star
Screeching tyre
Oooh, aahh.

Bang, crack, pop
Fizzle, spark hiss
Showers of sparks
Droplets of fire.

Fizzling frazzling frenzy
Overpowered supernova
Blooming flowers of streaming light . . .
Begin to fade . . .

Remnants of lost sparks
Simmer gently on
Fade slowly; slowly
'Til nothing is there.

Luke Edward Hayward (12)
King Edward VI School, Stratford-Upon-Avon

ILLUMINATION

Like a flicker of hope in a dark room,
Like a diamond in a beggar's cup,
Light floods life with happiness
And fills a depressed world with love.

Although sorrow brings us down,
Light is the hand that helps us back up.
Shards of joy piercing a cloud of worry,
Splinters of love, faith and eternal peace.

Light is a rainbow of harmony and delight,
Soaking even the darkest of thoughts in colour,
A lantern guiding the lost and downtrodden,
Assisting them on cold, winter nights.

The sparkle of stars in the eerie night's sky,
The beam of the moon as it hangs up high,
The warm tickling of a beautiful sun's rays,
As it cuddles you on a warm summer's day.

Illumination is everywhere,
For from the tranquil sky and from the luscious land,
Through an open door and through a crystal clear window,
Glorious colour seeps into our lives.

Adam Nash (12)
King Edward VI School, Stratford-Upon-Avon

THE SIGHT

Fire, fire, burning light,
Quickly flickering with a lot of might,
Challenging the wood to a fearsome fight,
Fiery flames, amazing sight.

How it is never blight,
Carry on shimmering at night,
Keeping me up to make me write,
As I watch this glorious sight.

Heera Johal (13)
King Edward VI School, Stratford-Upon-Avon

EXCALIBUR

The blade shines, majestic, bathing in the blue moonlight
Glistening greatly in the dark midnight sky
Lighting up rocks and fields with its power
Men gasp in awe, dumbstruck by the power
Animals flee in all directions
This is the power of Excalibur.

Before, it lived in a cave, waiting for the taste of blood
Revenge on mankind it wanted until it saw the light
Light enlightened the darkness
Darkness is no more.

War brought it to the cave
All it could see was blood and hate
War was its life.

Soon it started to see happiness
A smile gave the damned blade light
No longer did it kill
But gave hope and life
Now, here it lays, shining in the moonlight.

Easwar Vivekanandan (12)
King Edward VI School, Stratford-Upon-Avon

PHASES

Light, the vital energy
Needing it to always see,

But in the absence of this light,
Shadows rule,
Burning night,
The fuel of nightmares,
The stuff of fears,
Quelling our inner selves.

But, at the flick of a switch,
A striking match,
The blink of an eye,
The light has returned,
The dark has fled,
Leaving only blinding dread.

But, in a moment of clarity,
We see the world as it should be
And, like the melting of the snow
Back into the darkness we shall go.

Ben Charlie Hepworth (13)
King Edward VI School, Stratford-Upon-Avon

FIRE

Sparks igniting a flickering flame,
A volcano of colour bringing hope to the shadow.
A dragon battling against the endless darkness,
Elegantly fragile in the blackness.

Flashing, glowing, sparkling, illuminating,
Flickering, gleaming - a super-nova of light.
Igniting the darkness with shining embers,
Dazzlingly majestic in the night.

A ray, a flare, a spear of brightness,
A shower of cinder stars.
A phoenix dancing on the wood,
Full of hopeful mightiness.

Until the spray of evil water,
Hits the sun's beautiful daughter.
A hiss, a splutter, an evil mutter -

All is dark.

All is black.

James Howitt (12)
King Edward VI School, Stratford-Upon-Avon

FIRE

Flaring and crackling, like a great dragon's breath
Flickering and flashing like a blade in the moonlight
Splitting the light from the dark in the midst of a storm
Aglow in the darkness
A beacon among the clouds
Seeing us through the dead of night
At the rebirth of the sun, not a cloud to be seen
The birds tweet, the deer run free
The storm has passed
The night has gone
Light has returned to the world.

Aaron Gurudeep Singh Sandhu (12)
King Edward VI School, Stratford-Upon-Avon

SUNSET

The stars they roam, among the sky,
Like a dominant emperor up on high.
The pristine sun, soon to die,
Darkness is near, darkness is nigh.

Brilliant flares, in the night,
Pastel colours shall ignite.
Waves of emotion, may take flight,
Darkness is near, darkness in sight.

Vivid flames, dancing low,
Embers spark, simmer and glow.
Vibrant rays, come and go,
Darkness is near, darkness will show.

Flickering shadows, burning strong,
The moon peeks out, wants to belong.
The sky is black, drowning out song,
Darkness is here, but darkness seems wrong.

Joseph Hussain (12)
King Edward VI School, Stratford-Upon-Avon

FIRE

Fire, fire burning bright
Glowing, flickering with all its might
Giving off a pungent ash
From a distance, it goes *flash*
Thermal energy radiating out
Water is fire's only doubt.

Fire, fire raging on
Boldly and valiantly blazing on
Through forest and field
Leaving no yield
Then came the pouring rain
Dampening the fire in vain.

Nilay Sah (13)
King Edward VI School, Stratford-Upon-Avon

55

LIGHTNING

White flashes across dark, empty space
Bringing quick bursts of phosphorous glow
That come, shooting through this place
Like luminous arrows, fired from a magic bow

A loud crackle disturbs the silence
With a deep, booming, thunderous sound
Bringing its warning of impending violence
Of the looming storm that's coming around

Over and over, again and again
Quick flashes stab at the landscape
Their presence is mesmerising for all men
And for some, there is no escape

And then
It is gone
The storm has passed
The calm is here.

William West (12)
King Edward VI School, Stratford-Upon-Avon

TOTEM

They stand, undivided, yet in isolation
Watching those who tread
Hundreds of rings on the cold, oak bodies
Large, round eyes staring at spectators
The oak statues have seen many wars
Tell me what you are thinking
Tell me of my fortunes
Tell me why guidance sent me down this path
Tell me of my danger
Tell me of my loss
Tell me of my death
Tell me why . . .

George Hale (12)
King Edward VI School, Stratford-Upon-Avon

ONLY IN POETRY

I only told you I loved you in my poetry,
But never in person.
I loved you in my head,
But never with my song.

You couldn't see what I wrote,
I loved you in what my poems say,
It's too late for you to read them;
Now this verse will see decay.

The ghost of you in what I write,
A beauty of words that comes from you.
I feel a sting in what I sing,
I write to a person I'll never read to.

My words never reached you,
And perhaps they never will,
But my poetry is my heartbeat
Which beats forever still.

Toby Lucas (18)
King Edward VI School, Stratford-Upon-Avon

RAPTURE

All men as silent sheep doth tread upon
such sands of soot as Israelites enslaved
in bitter toil, in mortar and brick.
Yet, might Yahweh not, nor El doth send
deliverance nor exodus, not salvation so quick.

'Neath steel staves, cogs and pistons grind
their burden borne by calloused hands of grime
but in their wearing work, no pity find
rejoice in suffering to ends divine.
Conception cleansed of intercourse
Perfection from the purest source
The one and true blessed premise
Hark!
From barren metal springs forth Genesis.

Kinuthia Gakonga (16)
King Edward VI School, Stratford-Upon-Avon

CAMPFIRE

So comforting,
So helping, so leading,
Warm and welcoming,
Flickering and crackling,
The glowing colours
Struggling against shadow,
Fighting with the dark.

Slowly, it dies,
Its heart of embers
Extinguished.
The darkness envelops
The sooty remains.
The fire has gone out
And with it, light.

Lewis Briggs (12)
King Edward VI School, Stratford-Upon-Avon

LIGHT

An array of dazzling colours
Red, orange, yellow
Burning, burning.

I feel the heat on me
Warm, snug, safe
Sleeping, sleeping.

It blinds me
Glowing, blazing, shining
Hurting, hurting.

It has all gone now
Secure, safe, intact
Relieved, relieved.

Luke Groves (12)
King Edward VI School, Stratford-Upon-Avon

TOO MANY, TOO MUCH

A few more seconds, a few more *whys?*
A few more tears, a few more goodbyes.
No more laughter, no more cheer,
No more sunshine, only fear,
One more kiss, one more glance,
One more touch, one more dance.
A lot of seconds, a lot of *whys?*
A lot of tears, a lot of goodbyes.
Too much laughter, to much cheer,
Too many touches, not enough fear,
Too many kisses, too many glances,
Too much sunshine, too many dances.
Too much or too little, a lot less or a little less.
You are still gone and I remain a mess.
My words are all jumbled, my mind isn't clear,
Oh how I miss you so, if only you were here.

Liberty Royston (15)
King's College Alicante, Alicante

TRAPPED INSIDE A CAGE

Clearness,
Whiteness,
Perfection.

That's all I could see around me,
Even the darkest corner was pure,
As pure as the golden bars that formed my cage.

Brightness,
Blueness,
Fragility.

My wings fluttered, beaming with light,
As I tried to escape
From my golden paradise.

Submission,
Blackness,
Trapped.

My freedom, the stars,
The iron that made the bars,
The hope, the life,
That was cut with the butter knife.

Dreamlessness,
Goldenness,
Never-ending.

The story of a stolen butterfly,
So true, so charming.
Between the stakes that would take
All the blossoming away.

My nightmare,
My destiny,
My torture,
My future.

Aitana Cirauqui Palmero (13)
King's College Alicante, Alicante

WARRIOR

As a child you knew
you would act differently
you always listened
and followed intently
but you knew
deep inside
you would succeed
while they all hide
at night you would write
reams and reams
about a future world
but it would always make you scream
you never forgave, you never forgot
you knew it was wrong
no matter what they thought
all that work
you tried too hard
despite your efforts
the way is always barred
the broken shards
of your light-hearted soul
someone will find them
and you'll be under their control
it won't matter
even if it's your dream
you'll never escape them
it's just another of their schemes . . .

Kyla Watkins (13)
King's College Alicante, Alicante

WITHOUT THINKING

Without thinking,
today is the day, that's the day
that's the present. But should I say;
today is the day with the past of tomorrow.
Today was the future, your hope and your sorrow.

Because, thinking about it,
today is the day of tomorrow's yesterday.
The done and the doing however you may.
What is soon to be done is the new
tomorrow. Do I see tomorrow? Do you?

Now, thinking about it,
is there only ever a now?
A time we are conscious of how or
is that today? But what else should
I say?

Thinking about it,
today is the present, is now.
Its future is the past to be
shortly. It's tomorrow today and yesterday.
Yesterday was then, but was today and
tomorrow. Today's past is the future tomorrow.

But, without thinking,
today is the day that's the day
that's the present. Today is the day
and I like it that way.

Laura Warlow (14)
King's College Alicante, Alicante

ALONE

Here I am, shrivelled on the floor
when my dad's out there, in the war.
All I have is my empty bowl
and my rapidly vanishing, heartbroken soul.

He's out there, in the field, risking his life
whilst I'm sat down here, in a corner, in Fife.
I want him back, I want to help,
But the thought of war makes me yelp.

My clothes are ripped and badly torn
and now it freezes when it reaches dawn.
I said I would wait for him, it is our plight
and now I stay alive because of my might.

Mother left one day, but hasn't yet returned
and every day I grow more concerned.
Now I have to scavenge for my food,
but if someone sees, I am quickly shooed.

She said that she left because she had a plan,
I knew it was wrong, I wasn't a fan.
An old friend she once helped owed her one,
so she travelled the distance and now she's gone.

My mum and my dad will come back one day
and that will be the day I shout hooray!
But until that time, I am left alone,
With no one to hear my lengthening groan.

Grace Elizabeth Brown (13)
King's College Alicante, Alicante

WHAT CAN I SAY?

What can I say
about my first day?
It was in the morning,
when I started worrying.

What if people call me names
or don't include me in their games?
Wouldn't it be embarrassing
not knowing anything?

I attended school,
feeling like a fool.
Had no clue
of what to do.

People looked at me,
people pointed at me,
people pulled nasty faces at me,
but one girl waved at me.

She was Grace,
the girl with the best grades.
She always wore a smile,
which lasted more than a while.

In the end,
she became my friend.
What can I say
about the girl who lightened up my day?

Raquel Garrido Morales (13)
King's College Alicante, Alicante

IMMORTAL

We are all immortal
Until the day we die.
A bird is not a bird
Until the day it can fly.
No one is human
Until the day they cry.

If we are immortal
Then why can we die?
If a bird isn't a bird
Then how can it fly?
If we are all human
Then why must we cry?

Because, no immortal
Can live forever.

So live every moment,
Love every moment,
Like an immortal who can never die,
Like a bird learning to fly,
Like a person who has never cried.

After all,
We are immortal.

Ellen Warlow (16)
King's College Alicante, Alicante

LOST, BUT NOT LONELY . . .

As lonely as you think my life may be,
It's truly on the contrary if you ask me.
Down here far beneath the serene, topaz waves,
I am submerged here, for quite a long stay.
As the fish swim over, I am still alive.
Waiting to be uncovered so that I can live my life,
Shining through my greatest glory, I will survive.
Then one day, a boat came by
And two little men came swimming on by.
They looked around, I wondered why,
Until eventually, I caught their eye.
I rose and I rose until I came in contact with the sky,
There the sun gleamed, a golden glow
And I was on my way to somewhere I didn't know.
I preferred my old life under the sea,
I always seemed happy and filled with glee.
Now I'm stuck in a case of such,
Being stared at by passers-by.
I do not like this life very much,
Oh, someone please set me free.

Kirsty Ann Young (13)
King's College Alicante, Alicante

BOOKDRAGON

Reading was all she ever did,
Behind the oak tree's where she hid.
Reading her books all night and day,
Fiction worlds would take her away.

When tired of reality,
She dove into her fantasy.
Tearing through the yellowed pages,
Travelling back through the ages.

Tess Van Duijvenbode (14)
King's College Alicante, Alicante

OUT OF FEAR

The rain is pouring while I cry
my head is down, my heart is dry.
The little drops that touch my hand
leave me shaking where I stand.

I close the door and go to bed
I wake up as the living dead.
My face is pale, my skin is weak,
my mouth is pushed against my cheek.

Those are the shadows upon my back
I start to sense I'm under attack.
So I take a deep breath and here I am
same place, same time, same broken plan

I alight the bus to face them again
trembling as I drop my pen.
I can't take this anymore
too many worries to ignore.

I save my tears for another day
immersed again in work and play.

Justina Lipman (13)
King's College Alicante, Alicante

DAD

Your heart is like a chocolate fountain that never ends,
You're a warm sun, always warming me up, every time I'm cold,
You're like a doctor when I'm ill, you give me the right treatment,
You're my umbrella when it rains,
You're like a tiger that always loves clutches,
You're like a clown, always making me happy and making me laugh,
You're like a super auto TT the way you run
And you always wait for me.

You are one in a million!
I love you so, so much.

Amy Palfrey (12)
Lewis Girls' Comprehensive School, Hengoed

DARK THOUGHTS

My heart is as black as the night sky above.
My soul is grey, like stone,
My feelings are a rock that people like to throw away,
I am a shadow that no one will know.

My scars show hate,
My cuts show that I'm not loved,
My body shows pain that I feel,
My life is a movie, it will end.

I am loved by no one,
And I'm just a shadow
That no one will know,
Or am I just a speck of dust?

I sit in the dark,
All on my own,
No one to hug me,
No one to love me.

I am fed up,
I am frustrated,
I am hated,
I am no one.

I think it's time for me to say goodbye,
For me, I am dead,
No one will know
That I'm gone . . .

Goodbye . . .

Siâna Ahron (13)
Lewis Girls' Comprehensive School, Hengoed

MY SISTER

Every day, I wake up to the sun
And I know the day is going to be fun

Although I have an older sister
Who is more like a grumpy, old mister

Her name is Poppy
She can be quite stroppy

But anyway,
I truly love her so

She's a busy bee
Much busier than me

She always tries to revise
And ends up pulling out her eyes

She is very stressful
She should be more restful
A break is what she needs

Fair play to her, she is a fighter
Even though she could be lighter

I don't mind how she is
I just know that I love her.

Tilly Miller
Lewis Girls' Comprehensive School, Hengoed

OH PIZZA

Oh pizza,
how I love you,
your various toppings,
your tomato base.

Oh pizza,
my mealtimes wouldn't be great
if you weren't on the plate,
your cheese is the best,
pepperoni is as spicy as can be.

Oh pizza,
you're as yummy as a cake,
hot or cold,
Pizza Hut or Domino's,
Asda or Tesco,
you'll always be my favourite food.

Kasey Elysha Jordan Morris (12)
Lewis Girls' Comprehensive School, Hengoed

WHY?

Why?
Why do you have to be so far away?
Why do you have to have her?
Why? Why?

Do you?
Do you really want her?
Do you not want to be with me?
Do you?
Do you?

I've waited and waited
All of my life
For you . . .
And for you only!

Caitlin Rose Young
Lewis Girls' Comprehensive School, Hengoed

FOOD MORE LIKE FRUIT

Oh satsuma,
you are as close to me as any diamond,
but when I eat you, you're sour
and you hit me with your power.
but it is you I want to devour.
When I am in the garden to smell a flower,
you are there,
I think my new favourite fruit
is a pear.
My mum walks out there to try a plum,
'No Mum, do not be a bum!'
Oh Pear, I love you lots,
only if you don't stick me in a flower pot!

Megan Gray
Lewis Girls' Comprehensive School, Hengoed

ELEPHANTS

The elephant is big, strong and tall,
always hungry, eating more food an all,
they always have to scramble looking for more
and even, sometimes, trying to get in the store!

You'll always know when they're coming,
since you'll always hear their footsteps drumming,
they always like to travel in herds
and on their backs they carry birds.

Tree bark, fruit, bushes and twigs,
but you never know they might eat figs,
as night-time comes they go to rest,
and after all the food they've had they're probably blessed!

Alix Greenway
Lewis Girls' Comprehensive School, Hengoed

MY BED

I lay with my bae,
on Valentine's Day.

I rest my head
on my beautiful bed.

Oh bed, oh bed,
My bae, my bed.

When I come home from school,
I lay on your pillow and drool.

Bed, oh bed,
I love you, bed.

Ruby Anderson
Lewis Girls' Comprehensive School, Hengoed

WHEN I LOOKED INTO HIS EYES

When I looked into his eyes,
Oh his eyes, as blue as the skies.
His hair as blonde as a sunset,
His smile as big as can be.
When I looked into his eyes,
Oh his eyes, as blue as the sea.
His cheeks are as red as a rose,
Then I looked into his eyes,
Oh, his eyes as blue as can be.

Sophie Ann Phillips
Lewis Girls' Comprehensive School, Hengoed

TRICKING AND TREATING

(Lipogram - O)

Tricking and treating,
much sweetie eating,
dressed up little kids,
as vampires and pumpkins.

Egging cars,
watching stars,
singing creepy tunes at night,
you might get a fright.

I haven't a fear,
unless a witch is near,
Walking past gates,
staying up late.

Katie Lynn (12)
North Coast Integrated College, Coleraine

NYMPH

The nymph sits in the middle of the clearing,
The small human nearing,
Thousands of little droplets fall from the skies,
The girl could not be quiet, no matter how she tries.

She dances among the glowing tears,
That fall from every inch of the skies near,
The rainbow falls upon the two,
Colours of red, violet and blue,
The droplets glow with an unfading light,
As the nymph creeps back into the night.

This is now called the Dark Wood,
The reason our world is deprived of magic,
If only we could change it, if only we could . . .

Caitlin McGill (12)
North Coast Integrated College, Coleraine

CANDLELIGHT

Candlelight, what a lovely show,
flickering lights,
shimmer in darkness,
each one representing
hope and spirit.
Each making heat and light, but only
one for me; the one shining brightest in front of me -
the one who is always happy and smiling.
My darling candle, show me a path!
Where does that path lead?
Into my heart and hers.

Tyler Twaddle (13)
North Coast Integrated College, Coleraine

AUTUMN

Open the door to Heaven,
Open the door to branches on an old oak,
Open the door to a whirlwind of colour,
Red, brown, yellow, gold,
Open the door to a fire starved of its smoke,
Open the door to every crunch of leaves,
Every bit of wind that threatens to sweep you,
Every light,
Open your door to life,
Open your door to autumn.

Grace Wilson (13)
North Coast Integrated College, Coleraine

A WALK UP SNAEFELL

The mist settled on the hills, as I trudged on across the stony earth,
Ahead, a rabbit bounded across the path in front of me and through
the mist I could just see a handful of white dots in the valley below.

As I neared the summit,
I stopped and turned around to admire the view.
On my left was England and on my right was Ireland.
When I turned back round again,
I was greeted by a small number of sheep,
They immediately ran off.

I carried on through the damp, cold air, until I met a white mountain
hare,
It looked like it had started to moult,
Clumps of hair just hanging from its frail, limp body.

I continued on my journey with only a few metres to the peak of this
great mountain,
I could now fully see the shape of the cafe and the railings leading to
the very top and I couldn't wait to get a nice warm hot chocolate.

The mountain tram had arrived, ready to take people back, just as I
ordered my drink,
I was now at the highest point on the Isle of Man,
A whole 620 metres covered on foot and now it was time to depart.

I climbed onto the 100-year-old mountain tram and waited for the
driver to come and start us off on our passage back to Laxey.
The tram screeched to life and we had begun.

I closed my eyes and tried to remember everything I had come across
today,
The last thought that came to mind was the view.
All of the United Kingdom in front of me and nothing standing in my
way.

Amy Ratcliffe (12)
Ramsey Grammar School, Isle Of Man

ONE DAY I'M PLAYING HAPPILY

One day, I'm playing happily
Next day, I'm fleeing with my family
Crying, shouting, when will it ever end?
Bombs, blasts, no way to defend.

For days on end we roam
Because we have no such thing as home
We have no place to stay
Will we live another day?

We jump into the little boat
Will we sink or will we float?
Rowing along in the deep, dark sea
Can't wait to get off, then I'll be free

I look out and see land ahead
And a small figure, probably dead
He was washed up on shore, suffocated by the sea
His mother devastated, wouldn't you be?

I travel through Europe, I enjoy all the sights
Better than being at home with all the fights
Calais in the distance, thousands of people
We all have had to fight the same battle

We're not accepted, not treated right
Until finally, Britain see the light
Now we all have roofs over our heads
And we can enjoy a night in a nice comfy bed

This is my story, this is my journey
I am a refugee.

Georgia Keggin (12)
Ramsey Grammar School, Isle Of Man

THE SEASIDE

On the first day of the holidays
I went down to the sea.
I strolled onto the beach and was confronted
By a big gust of sea air and a lung-full of salt.
All I could hear was the sound of the waves
Beating on the beach and the pebbles and the cliffs.

The birds sang,
A hard song of cries and squawks.
I climbed among the sharp rocks and pools
And gazed towards the sea.
Brightly coloured fish of all shapes and sizes swam
Without a care or fear.

I looked again and saw,
Beautiful sea urchins waving in the tide.
The shape of tall and mighty cliffs
Standing powerful and majestic,
Soaring towards the sky.
Seagulls circling their nests on rocky cliffs,
A pod of dolphins swimming strongly,
Fast, against the outline of the hot and fierce sun.

On the last day of the holidays,
I returned to my home and was confronted
By traffic, fumes and pollution
And the sound of engines and city people,
Heading to the high rise office blocks in the sky.

Oscar Jackson (11)
Ramsey Grammar School, Isle Of Man

THE EVIL SPIRIT

The night falls and you're about,
You prance and pry without a doubt.
Though you are the spirit, you created the screams,
Thou art the one who ruins hopes and dreams.

The soul and heart are imprisoned and forever alone,
No one dares to ever step into your zone.
The silence creeps through the graveyard, cold,
Leaving air as thick as ancient mould.

We sit in our houses with dread and worry,
Scared of where you'll strike next, our hearts beat with hurry,
Because with your heart as cold as solid rock,
We know you come out and play at the 12th strike of the clock.

The air outside is cold and crisp,
With the wind howling, making leaves dance and twist,
Only one creature stalks around so fast,
Thee whom we call Evil Spirit of present and past.

The light you take, the fears you make,
The deathly silence that you create,
With your cloak, as thick as Manannan's mist,
You have to target us, you cannot resist.

As yet again darkness looms over town and city,
You find a way to scare without compassion or pity,
Your tactics of fright have no limit,
Oh you are the one known as the Evil Spirit!

Eleanor Elizabeth Corrin (13)
Ramsey Grammar School, Isle Of Man

AUTUMN

The first crimson leaf drifts off the old oak tree,
Gently floating through the air,
Landing on the crisp, green, frost-tipped grass,
Autumn is coming.

Many shades of red and territories of brown,
Smother the forest floor, crunching underfoot,
Squirrels dart up trees, collecting acorns,
Autumn is here.

The cold air bites the tip of your nose,
Howling winds toss the bare branches of trees,
Pounding rain clatters on the windows,
Autumn is chilly.

Great beauty and bright berries,
The vibrant colours of the leaves,
The delicate dew and translucent blue skies,
Autumn is beautiful.

Warm coat and gloves,
Pumpkin spice lattes,
Hats, scarves and fluffy socks,
Autumn is cosy.

The first flake of snow drifts through the air,
Delicately landing on the tip of my finger,
It melts and vanishes quickly,
Winter is coming.

Anna Elizabeth Lashley (12)
Ramsey Grammar School, Isle Of Man

THE ECHO OF THE TRIBES

Darkness,
routine,
a way of life repeated
over and over again.

The grass, sharp as knives,
the leaves, withering away.

We grow up, taught how to fend for ourselves
and yet nothing changes,
apart from the days.

Sewing, hunting, changing, giving.
It all means
nothing,
after the iron teeth shred our beautiful nature.
It means nothing
when life dies.

We give life, we take life, we help life, we harm life.
It was still worth nothing.
Unknown,
forgotten.

In the end we have lived; no one knew we were there.
We pass away, leaving nothing,
just the echoes of our past.

Ealish Withington (12)
Ramsey Grammar School, Isle Of Man

THE TRICKING FREAK

On Monday I told my brother it was bank holiday,
he believed me and did not turn up to school that day.
His teacher Miss Bolt asked me where he was,
I said to her, 'I haven't got a clue' even though this wasn't true.

On Tuesday I tricked my cousin Millie into thinking she was ever so silly,
she is only two and thought it was true,
then she went off crying, *boo hoo, boo hoo.*

On Wednesday I tricked my friend Lillie May into thinking it was show and tell today,
as gullible as she was she brought in a box of frogs,
the teacher was mad and rang her dad.

On Thursday I tricked my older sister Lexi to thinking her boyfriend was cheating with her bestie,
she ran out the room and screamed, 'I'm gonna sort him soon!'

Later that day I opened my front door to find the people I tricked standing on my living room floor,
they were very angry and upset,
they accepted my apology,
though it will be something they will never forget.

I regret everything I did that week,
now everybody calls me The Tricking Freak!

Natalie Sewell (12)
Ramsey Grammar School, Isle Of Man

THINKING OF YOU

I smile on the outside, but nobody knows
I may seem happy, but I am broken
Thoughts of pain and despair swirl through my mind
My soul faded years ago
I sit here, wearily, wearing this mask
Hiding my true self from reality
I want to change what I am
Be who I pretend to be
But I know that I can't, I never will
I'm stuck this way forever
Drowned in darkness and oblivion
Abandoned by the blissful person I used to be
I don't understand joy - not anymore
Instead, I'm surrounded by gloom
My inner lamp has completely burned out
Never to be set alight again
Nothing is the same - not in this state
Where they are filled with optimism, I am empty
It's your fault that I'm like this, that I'm dead inside
But you couldn't have known, no one could predict
I sit like this every day of my life
Hour upon hour, thinking of you.

Freya Melvin (12)
Ramsey Grammar School, Isle Of Man

HOCKEY POEM

Hockey is fun, interesting and a good sport, then you score and shout
and cheer.
The people who win are the people who play fair, by not disobeying
the rules.
When you play, you chase the ball round and round to score a goal,
You defend the goal to save the ball, to save the ball, to save the goal
And by playing the game you have some fun, you may win by playing
fair.

Caitlin Corkill (11)
Ramsey Grammar School, Isle Of Man

ANIMAL ABUSE

Innocent animals left on the street,
They have no family to stay with,
Tortured and ignored, with nothing to eat,
They think they have no purpose to live.

People beat them with whips and sticks,
They feel all rejected and forlorn inside,
Until they become really ill and sick,
Those humans have no frame of mind.

They are left alone,
All cold and sad,
They whine, cry and moan,
'This is really, really bad!'

Why do they have to go through this?
Please answer my question,
They deserve a big hug and kiss
And don't want all this depression.

They are like humans too, you know,
Please don't treat them differently,
They may not be able to talk, so,
Please, just handle them gently.

Victoria Rose Watson (12)
Ramsey Grammar School, Isle Of Man

LIFE

Thinking life is simple,
Is the worst mistake you can make,
The good and the bad ripple,
The easy and the hard ache.

You may feel like you have a curse,
You may feel like you don't matter,
But things have to get worse
Before they can get better.

Emma Wilkinson (12)
Ramsey Grammar School, Isle Of Man

MY THREE DOGS

Barney is an old dog, but he's very wise,
His fur is red and gold and shines like his eyes.
Drummer is a young dog, full of life and fun,
He comes hurtling towards you when you shout, 'Drum!'

But my favourite dog is Pepper,
She has four legs to walk about.
A tail that dangles at one end
And on the front she has a snout.

She sometimes comes when whistled,
But quite often she does not.
So I often think and wonder,
What sort of ears she's got.

She sleeps upon the sofa,
But sometimes on my bed.
But when she dreams she quivers
And tramples on my head.

But, despite her mighty fidgets
And the bruising that I got,
I love my little Pepper,
Not a bit but quite a lot.

Erin Callow (12)
Ramsey Grammar School, Isle Of Man

THE STRUGGLE

Life is a handful for so many people,
Being bullied from young can be a norm,
Have you ever felt you are the ball on the pitch,
Being kicked round endlessly, until punctured?
Life is a mystery waiting to be solved,
But sometimes it isn't,
That's what life is about.

Hannah Stafford (12)
Ramsey Grammar School, Isle Of Man

THE MOONLIGHT DANCE

I woke up with a start
By feet touching the light green hairs of the Earth
The moonlight gently touched my face
Its silver shine filled the room with joy

The lady I saw was dancing
She twirled and twirled, round and round
Up she went to the stars
Higher she went, the more curious I felt

I stepped outside, the gold grass sent a shiver
She moved swiftly and carefully
Up the light she went
Her silver dress and hair followed her graceful movements.

I watched her, up she went
She was on the full moon,
Dancing beautifully until the sunrise

Every night I waited to see her
To see what she was or where she was
I never saw her
But I will never forget her moonlight dance.

Reese Dalugdugan (12)
Ramsey Grammar School, Isle Of Man

THE LUCKY BOOTS

The boy thinks his boots are lucky,
His mates think he's mad,
But he's not that bad,
He's through, on goal
And scores with his left toe!

He grew out of his boots
And was worried his luck would change,
If only he knew it was his skill, not luck,
That made the team win the cup!

Abbie Callow (12)
Ramsey Grammar School, Isle Of Man

85

THE COAST

The coast is a marvellous place,
As the wind rushes past my face
I wonder at the power of the ocean,
Dancing in natural motion.

At the Ayres the seals
look at you like you are their meals,
They look so cute you have to stay,
But then they go off and play.

The animals glide free
As they stare at me,
The birds jump off their perch
As for fish they start to search.

The waves crash and bang,
They creep up like a gang,
They hit the cliff with so much force,
They destroy everything in their course.

The coast will forever last,
You can see the present and the past,
It changes over time,
But is always at its prime.

Jack Christian (11)
Ramsey Grammar School, Isle Of Man

REMEMBRANCE

The people who fight,
The courage they hold,
The fire they light,
Their medals were gold.

With bravery and ambition,
They all enlisted,
Dodging German ammunition,
'Over the top boys!' they insisted.

And how they will be evoked,
After their uphill battle,
Our memories of them provoked,
As the commemoration guns rattle.

The poppies that mark,
The wars gone by,
They fly with the larks,
As we watch the sky.

So remember, remember,
They fought for us, then lay,
On the 11th November,
So we can have our today.

Ben Johnston (12)
Ramsey Grammar School, Isle Of Man

THE WORLD

The world could be so much better
From wars, thirst, hunger and disease,
Put your technology down, try writing a letter,
People are starving, they'd do anything for cheese.

Hungry children and adults too,
We have more than enough, so why aren't they getting any?
We can all make a change, I'm talking to you,
Distribute it fairly, we could save many.

Greedy politicians, they all want power,
They can make the world better and make a change,
Yet they do nothing and watch from their tower,
So get out your seats, stop playing Candy Crush, stop being deranged.

Illness, disease, so many have passed,
The NHS has turned down many
Poor people who can't afford it, we could have let them last,
They've turned children away, it's uncanny.

We can all make change, together,
Let's make the world last forever.

Anna Tramontana (12)
Ramsey Grammar School, Isle Of Man

DO YOU HAVE A BEST FRIEND?

Best friends, you can't beat them,
You don't always have to keep them,
Even if they annoy you,
It doesn't mean that you are through.

You two will be together forever,
All the way to the end.

Someone to never, ever forget,
Do you have a best friend?

Caitlin Skillan (12)
Ramsey Grammar School, Isle Of Man

YOU DON'T NEED TO BE A PRINCESS

I don't need money
Not just being funny,
No complications
No explanations,
Talking is not needed
With you, I'm just speechless,
So I'm falling for you now
And I don't need a crown.
Because I'm not a princess
I'm just a girl,
It's every woman for herself
In this world,
No complications
No explanations,
Just you and me, tonight,
Just you and me, tonight.

Amber Olivia Black (11)
Ramsey Grammar School, Isle Of Man

THE MAN ON THE HORSE

There he rides, the man on the horse,
His voice was rough and coarse,
He seemed so high up,
Way out of my league
And people used to tell me
He's not as bad as he seemed.
It was love at first sight,
But I was scared of the height,
What if I fell? Fell to Hell?
I decided to stay with myself of course,
Not riding along
With the man on the horse.

Regan Dakin (12)
Ramsey Grammar School, Isle Of Man

MUSIC

Music is freedom,
A chance to get away,
It's addictive and relaxing,
You could listen all day.

There are songs that are true, they tell no lies,
Things from experience, people shared and did not hide.
Music can change you, it has helped through tough times,
You must believe me, it will make you feel alive.

There are so many types, one is waiting for you,
You'll be a better person if you make the right move,
No one is above you, nobody below,
The choice is yours, I gave it a go.

There'll be songs you hate, songs that you can't stand,
But there will always be a right one on hand.
So trust me and make a note of this,
Music can change you, so don't give it a miss.

Alex Yardley (13)
Ramsey Grammar School, Isle Of Man

SUMMER DAYS

Leaves blowing in the breeze,
Bees buzzing in the trees.
Birds singing, sweet but strong,
Eating worms, one by one.

Children laugh, dance and play,
Making noises all night and day.
Farmers harvesting, making food,
Milking cows, the ones that mooed.

Night has come, the sun is down,
All is quiet, not a sound.
Tomorrow it will start once more,
Lots more fun and that's for sure.

Kitty Treanor (11)
Ramsey Grammar School, Isle Of Man

90

WEAR A POPPY

Wear a poppy on this day
On the eleventh day, stand and pray
Think about those who died
And all the people who cried.

Wear a poppy on this day
Have two minutes' silence, then say
Well done to those who held a gun
Until the deadly war was won

Wear a poppy on this day
For several minutes stop your play
When we had great power
They fought till their very last hour

Wear a poppy on this day
On the eleventh day, stand and pray
Think about those who lost their lives
In Flanders Fields.

Abigail McGovern (11)
Ramsey Grammar School, Isle Of Man

STRAWBERRY JAM

Strawberry jam, a taste so sweet,
enough to make a cake complete.
Spread it on bread, spread it on toast,
tastes as good as a Sunday roast!

First comes the fruit, the red delight,
the bright, vibrant red, what a sight!
Then with sugar, into the pot,
don't touch it yet, it's too hot!

Left to cool on the window sill,
then to the store, to reach the till.
Three pounds, four pounds, too much for me;
you can grow strawberries just for free!

Benjamin Li (12)
Ramsey Grammar School, Isle Of Man

THE SEASONS

Spring...
Blossom trees swaying in the wind, baby bunnies bouncing on the grass,
Crisp, frosty mornings and sweet little snowdrops we pass.

Summer...
Birds singing a sweet song, the smell of freshly cut grass,
Swimming when it's too warm, followed by the collection of sea glass.

Autumn...
The sound of rain falling, crunching through brightly coloured fallen leaves,
Finding conkers, dressing up in ghoulish wear to celebrate All Hallows' Eve!

Winter...
Snow and ice, clear nights and starry skies,
Snuggling with hot chocolate under a warm purple blanket,
Christmas and brightly wrapped packages - surprise!

Olivia Abraham (11)
Ramsey Grammar School, Isle Of Man

THE FYSKOOGLE

You may have heard a poem like this before,
Written by a poet who I think is quite a bore,
So I'm gonna write a poem better than the poem before.

The Fyskoogle, a monster, came to town one day,
Called the Fyskoogle, it prowled the streets eating all the plums it saw,
Nobody knows why, but it has a craving for plums,
But one day, it ate somebody's mum!
Soon enough, everyone decided to run
From the Fyskoogle who started drinking rum...

Nobody has seen the plum-eating, mum-eating, drunken Fyskoogle since...

Sam Rodick (12)
Ramsey Grammar School, Isle Of Man

THE BILLOWS

She has one of those pretty face
wings on her eyeliner that will take her places.
Her hair's so soft that her head's in the clouds
but I'd rather be there than where I am: the ground.
I'm riddled with worms, the birds and the bees
harassed by children and their scabby knees -
yet she manages to giggle and retain her poise
oblivious or remiss to the hideous noise.

How she still smiles, I'm left to wonder,
even as her clouds rain and thunder.
It pours, it roars, it gets you down,
but she's resilient, when I'd simply drown.

She's unaware, which saves her time,
from fretting over yesterday's crimes,
she's untroubled, so dreadfully carefree,
how wonderful to not be like me.

Tara Brown (17)
Ramsey Grammar School, Isle Of Man

SKY

Stretching out, far above,
Covering the world in a blanket of love.
From east to west and north to south,
Giving oxygen to everyone's mouth.
Keeping warmth on a bright sunny day,
Bringing in rain to spoil our play.
I don't like the sky when it's grey,
It leaves me wishing for the dawn of another day.
Changing colours, full of light,
Making every day happy and bright.

Sarah Vondy (12)
Ramsey Grammar School, Isle Of Man

LIFE

Life can be difficult if
you do not try new things.

The grass is green
and the sky is blue,
it all awaits for me and you.

There's a beautiful world ahead of you,
go out and explore,
the world is full of adventures,
all waiting to be found.

Find a hobby you enjoy,
running, swimming, tennis, more
anything you can explore.

Don't stop living each day,
keep having fun until
the next day is due in its place.

Kaitlin Airey (13)
Ramsey Grammar School, Isle Of Man

MY SUMMER CHILDHOOD

Walking by the small waves,
Peeking in the big caves,
Picking up seaside shells,
Listen to the seagull's tell
Their adventures to Timbuktu,
While the pigeons go coo, coo.
The wet sand between my toes,
Everyone definitely knows,
An ice cream in my hand,
Oops! I dropped it in the sand.
Oh what fun it is to be a child,
Even though we do go wild!

This is my childhood.

Siân Hooson-Owen (11)
Ramsey Grammar School, Isle Of Man

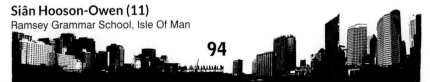

POOR AND THE RICH

The wind blew
As the birds flew,
Over the bright blue sky.

People were dying,
Whilst the rich are flying
And the orphan children crying.

We should stop this now,
Don't take a bow,
It's not your show.

Why is this happening?
They shouldn't have to suffer,
We are all equal.

Let's show what we can do,
As the war continues
And more people's lives are ruined.

Ethan Hignett
Ramsey Grammar School, Isle Of Man

YOU LOVE ME

You brought me sunshine
When I saw rain,
You brought me laughter
When I felt pain.

You cared
When no one else did,
Two careless souls became one,
You don't care about my imperfections.

I love you!

Hannah Kniveton (11)
Ramsey Grammar School, Isle Of Man

NO NEED TO BE PERFECT

Maybe it is
Maybe it isn't
You're not always right when wrong comes to visit.
Maybe it's big
Maybe it's small
All good things happen to those of us all.
Maybe it's smart
Maybe it's dumb
It'll be worth it, just let it have fun.
Maybe it's perfect
But nobody's perfect!
But all of these things, when corrected
Make up you
Not everything has to be perfected.

Just be you
Because yourself to me is perfect!

Alice Violet Huxham (11)
Ramsey Grammar School, Isle Of Man

MAYHEM

Look, look over there, a white and spotty dog
no it's not, it's over there, now it's in the courts
it galloped down through the yard
into the rooms, 'Oh please don't eat my work!'
Then it went into the rest room,
Oh my goodness, it has an Afro.

Ding dong, ding dong,
'Goodbye my dog, you made my day,
I hope I made your white and spotty day too.'

Lukas Hickey (12)
Ramsey Grammar School, Isle Of Man

STAR

My glimmering light shines down on the hurting Earth,
Brings peace and hope to a wonderful new birth.
People with anger and hate look up at my silver light
With hope in their eyes, burning bright.

I sometimes feel lonely sat up there in the sky
And wish I could meet the hate and anger and stare them in the eye.

I watch all through the darkness of every blessed night,
When my fiery core shines so very bright,
At such a faraway and abandoned height.

My peaceful light will one fateful day go out,
Falling through the universe, without a flying doubt,
But I always hope my seemingly warm and loving presence
Has left the hurting Earth with an almighty difference,
Even to one curious soul,
Who would have felt my shimmer, to have met its goal.

Isla May Hampton (11)
Ramsey Grammar School, Isle Of Man

AUTUMN

Leaves, yellow, orange and red,
Falling from the tree, is the tree dead?
Thick, heavy brambles, spiky and green,
Heavy with black fruit, lots can be seen.

Dark, clear, cold nights,
Smoky chimneys, all the houses are alight,
Sunsets with colours that take breath away,
Can't quite believe it's the end of the day.

Fright night is near,
Ghosts and zombies cause fear,
Ginny the witch could give us a fright,
But with lots of sweets to eat
They soften the bite.

Elena Dimsdale (12)
Ramsey Grammar School, Isle Of Man

97

THEY SAY . . .

They say her hair is like the whistling wind,
They say her soul has never sinned.

They say her lips are red as blood,
They say her eyes twinkle as they should.

They say her heels make a thunderous crack,
They say her heart is a vortex of black.

They say her stare could instantly kill,
They say her hands are soft and still.

They say her nails are flawlessly painted,
They say her innocent mind has just been tainted.

They say her life has now no hope,
They say her conscience will never cope.

She proved *'they'* wrong!

Maisie Megson (12)
Ramsey Grammar School, Isle Of Man

NO-MAN'S-LAND

1917
Here we are in no-man's-land.
listening to the guns rattle,
Sounds just like a rattlesnake leaping into battle.
Can you smell the air, the deathly, dark air?
That is the sign of death creeping in to scare.
The souls and souls and souls,
Are being taken away,
From the barbed-wired no-man's-land
To the Heavens above to care.
The soldiers above, looking down on you are saying,
'Do it for your country, your country needs you too . . .'
Now the guns are silent and the battle has been won,
Now we can remember, now the dying is done.

Archie Kershaw (12)
Ramsey Grammar School, Isle Of Man

PEN PAL

Shall I compare thee to stationery
I said to my very best friend
Though not as bright as a dictionary
There is no harm to pretend

You're as honest and straight as a ruler
And much more useful than a pen
Like a calculator, you couldn't be cooler
So that scores you ten out of ten

You stick by me like the world's strongest glue
We never get overly stressed
Though this year, I haven't seen much of you
As a friend you're surely the best

I'm the pencil and you're the highlighter
I draw the world and you make it brighter.

Lily Byrne (12)
Ramsey Grammar School, Isle Of Man

REMEMBER, REMEMBER. A REMEMBRANCE POEM

Remember, remember, the 11th of November
Remember those who died
And those who survived

Remember, remember, the 11th of November
See them marching down the street
For what might be their last few feet

Remember, remember, the 11th of November
The men being shot in the trenches
And being remembered on their benches

Remember, remember, the 11th of November
Where the soldiers held their shields
Poppies now grow in Flanders Field.

Will Hassall (12)
Ramsey Grammar School, Isle Of Man

99

LIFE'S NOT A LOVE STORY

Once there was a girl called Lexi, who had a cat called Mexi.
Lexi liked a boy called Jason, who also had a curly cat called Mason.
Lexi heard that Jason and Mason walked in the streets, so Lexi followed.
The next day, Jason and Lexi went to school and she followed him everywhere.
They saw each other at the school dance and Lexi made herself look pretty,
They walked closer and closer, until Jason spoke.
Lexi was so excited, over the moon in fact,
She tried to speak back, but what came out was not pretty;
Puke everywhere.
All over her suit and her dress.

The lesson of this story -
Life's not a love story.

Georgia Dobbie (11)
Ramsey Grammar School, Isle Of Man

I HATE YOU CANCER

I hate you, I hate you, why can't you see
How you took my heart and broke it,
When you took them from me?

She was my favourite aunt you see,
For only a short time
And then you came and took her
When she was in her prime.

She was there to lend a hand,
When you thought you had no one at all,
But that was till the day *you* came to call.

She suffered for so long
And was always in pain,
You took a beautiful woman
And made her die in vain.

Poppy Kennish (12)
Ramsey Grammar School, Isle Of Man

WAR POEM

Under the bunker
The cold, wet ground
My head starts to pound.
I wish I had a real bed and floor,
I can't take this anymore.
We hardly get any sleep
We sleep in the mud, why is it so deep?
The guns shoot - *bang!*
It's an early start, the pots go *clang.*
All there is for breakfast is water and bread,
I hardly managed to get out of bed.
It's Christmas time, we all have fun,
It's getting dark, down goes the sun,
Boxing Day, it's back to fighting . . .
Will this ever end?

Amy Rodick (11)
Ramsey Grammar School, Isle Of Man

NATURE

The wind blows though me like a spirit of its own accord,
it whispers as its soft, cold lips caress my ears.
I shiver and retreat back into the warmth of my man-made home,
Nature is my friend, my god and my being,

I would sit down for hours,
glaring at the sky, while the summer breeze gently blows
and the sun blazes its heat onto the Earth.

I'd rather hug a thousand trees than hug a single being,
for it doesn't scare me and it won't hurt me.
Nature takes its own course, growing wherever it can,
it is Nature's world, not ours for the taking.

Let Nature spread its wings, it claws and it leaves.
As it awakens to a new beginning every dawn.

Rochelle Jerrum-Dore (18)
Rye Studio School, Rye

102

DAYS OF THE WEEK

Monday is the worst,
When you are about to go mad,
You are too tired for anything,
It must be the worst day of the week.

Tuesday is OK,
You start to brighten up,
You go to the library as happy as Larry
And your smile is still there when you get home.

Wednesday is here,
The sky is nice and bright,
You can just sit in your chair
Talking to your best friend.

Thursday has come,
Only one more day left,
So when you get home
You plan your weekend ahead.

It's Friday,
The best day of the week,
It's the weekend now,
You get to do what you want.

Saturday is here,
You go pick up your friend,
Then you go to the movies
And just eat and eat and eat!

Now it's Sunday,
Not so good,
As tomorrow is Monday
And the week starts all over again.

Amy Rooney (12)
St Louis Grammar School, Newry

FIRE AND ICE

Once upon a time
Two young dragons had a tremendous fight,
Named Fire and Ice,
Fire was then put to sleep by Ice's might.

But, many millennia later,
Fire awakens, stretching his giant wings, then takes flight,
He descends upon the nearest village
And breathes his fiery breath with all his might.

A local harp player puts Fire to sleep,
As a blacksmith crafts a weapon,
That will give this monster a treat.

Ice takes up the blacksmith's sword
And delivers a final blow,
That leaves Fire floored.

The village can now sleep in peace,
As Fire's wrath is now deceased.

Chloe Hughes (12)
St Louis Grammar School, Newry

A HORSE RIDER'S LIFE

Hour and hours every day,
Around horses and ponies giving them hay,
Riding them out, seven days a week,
You can't wait to get some sleep.
Once you are done going in and out
And being out and about,
You really don't know where the day has gone.

The next day is here,
The sky is finally nice and clear,
A calm and peaceful hack up the lane
And you're ready for your day to start all over again.

Amy Rooney (12)
St Louis Grammar School, Newry

CHRISTMAS MORNING

I got up on Christmas morning when my alarm began to ring,
I rushed down the stairs as quick as I could to see what Father
Christmas did bring.
We walked into the living room excitedly, my dad turned on the light,
The room was covered with so many toys, what a wonderful sight!

I opened all the boxes, I couldn't believe what I got
And there, on the arm of the sofa was a letter I nearly forgot.
It told me to go to the garage, where there was one more surprise for
me,
I ran down the yard and I couldn't believe what I could see.

Two amazing quads, one was red and one was blue,
Dad said, 'The blue one is for me and the red one is for you.'
I was so surprised, I had to get the keys,
I went up the lane for a spin.
I was so happy, I couldn't believe it;
On my face was such a big grin!

Conall Rooney (12)
St Louis Grammar School, Newry

MY IDEA OF FUN!

Being whisked into the magical land of a book
If you want to come you have to have a look
Any time I want to go
I will open my book and I will do so

You can find your favourite band
Or maybe find yourself in a candy land
Every time I open my eyes
A new adventure will arise

Every day there is something new
Maybe the world is made of goo
Or maybe you are riding on a kangaroo
But this is all up to you!

Callum McHugh (11)
St Louis Grammar School, Newry

THE SEASONS

Summer, autumn, winter and spring
Don't get worried, it's an annual thing
The weather will change, yes, I know
If you watch it will come to show.

Wintertime
Wintertime is time for snow
To the south the birds shall go.

Springtime
In the springtime days grow warm
And for plants, new buds will form.

Autumn time
Now autumn is here the air is cool
And we must go back to school.

It's just like I said, summer, autumn, winter and spring,
Yes, it is, it's an annual thing.

Amy Cunningham (11)
St Louis Grammar School, Newry

CELEBRATION

Celebration is a time of joy and fun
Celebration is a time to meet family and friends
Celebration is a time for love and friendship
Celebration is a time to be kind to others
Celebration is a time for sharing
Celebration is a time to pray
But what really is celebration?

James Kelly (12)
St Louis Grammar School, Newry

AN ORIGINAL START

Oh how, again and again you ask for an
additional chance,
To take an original start,
An opportunity to blot out our faults
And transform our faults into winnings.
To build an original start,
It only asks for all of your soul,
So don't fall victim to anguish,
As tomorrow you can start again.

Lee Harper (12)
St Louis Grammar School, Newry

11 NO MORE

Eleven no more, I remember the day,
Doing what I want and being able to play,
It's hardly one hundred with wrinkles on my face,
Twelve is not so bad, but once I get older
I won't be able to tie my lace.
Life is timeless, that is once you're old,
My bones will shatter
And I'll be grumpy and cold.

Evan McLoughlin (12)
St Louis Grammar School, Newry

FAMILY LIFE

Family life is busy all the time,
It's fun this way, I wouldn't change mine,
Dad's out first, he leaves at seven,
But he stays up late, way past eleven.

Me and my brother get ready for school,
With Mum shouting, 'No electronics!' because that's the rule.

The clock ticks by, we must leave by eight,
Because we dilly-dally sometimes, we're late.

Mum's either in the salon or working at home,
When we're out the dog's all alone,
He sleeps all day, quiet as a mouse,
When we're all out, he guards the house.
That's his job, so that's all fine,
I love my dog, he's special and he's mine.

Lunchtime strikes, I can feel it in my belly,
I wish I was at home right now, watching the telly.

3:20 strikes and we're out the gates,
As I walk home, I say goodbye to my mates.
When we are all back, safe and sound,
Mum and Dad sigh as their feet touch the ground.

Mum tidies up and Dad cooks dinner,
Whilst I chill on the sofa, ha! I'm the winner.
Before I know it, it's getting late,
Mum says, 'Off to bed,' which I really hate.

I climb into bed, fast asleep I go,
When I hear Mum say, 'It's time to get up,'
'Urgh - I know!'

Darcie Howe (11)
St Wilfrid's RC School, Crawley

THE BATTLE OF BRITAIN

Flying in formation,
Charging at each other,
Experienced and unexperienced,
Some only a day trained,
But on red alert all the same.

Some of the birds fall,
Others stay high,
He needs to jump,
He needs to leave,
His wings are on fire!

A trail of smoke divides the sky,
As a white dot slowly lands,
A crash site on the edge of town,
A pilot wounded
And out of the fight.

The field that was so full,
Now barren,
Not a vehicle in sight,
Only the sound of drums,
Drums and cymbals,
That cost lives.

The brave pilots return,
But only half,
The rest, at peace,
These pilots fought to keep the land safe,
Who gave their lives for others.

Patrick Daly (11)
St Wilfrid's RC School, Crawley

GENERATIONS

Worldwide, we stand with pride
Linking arms, side by side
Unity with expectance
And repentance
All walls will crumble
Speak loud, don't mumble

Don't deny the charge
No matter what age
The world that you are making
Will never end up breaking
We are the change and we will fight
'Cause we, the world, can change overnight.

Kelsey Louise Norris (13)
St Wilfrid's RC School, Crawley

THE PINK MONTH

All people seem to care about this month is Halloween,
But there are illnesses that matter, but go unseen.
The priorities of this month we need to rethink,
Because what really matters this month, is the colour pink.

Not yellows or purples, or reds, blues or green,
Because pink stands for an organisation, a family and a team.
I have an important charity in mind, I'll give you a clue,
It could affect anyone, anywhere, maybe even you.

I'm talking about cancer, because research is key,
Any donation helps, no matter how much it may be.
So this month, value all that you have and be kind
And make sure that you have the pink month in mind.

Jodie O'Connor (14)
St Wilfrid's RC School, Crawley

A POEM ABOUT DANCE

Dance is a chance to let your imagination run free
It allows you to decide who you really want to be
The spins and the twirls make you forget for a while
The times you'd try to go the extra mile
Dance is something that will let you express
The way you feel, do you feel stressed?
Just think about dance as your number one chance
To show other people who it is you are
Relax, feel free, don't worry, don't stress
Don't feel like you need to impress
At least allow yourself to do your best
And forget about the rest.

Kirsty Sepenoo (12)
St Wilfrid's RC School, Crawley

WONDER

I wonder why, I look at the sky and wonder why?
The poor little boy I saw today
Begging and pleading all night and all day
His eyes were grey, hollow holes of sadness
Pouring into his soul

I wonder why, I look a
t the sky and wonder why?
Innocent people fleeing from countries to save their lives
The lives are shattered like broken glass
I wonder, wonder why?

Nicholatie Namatovu (11)
St Wilfrid's RC School, Crawley

GHOST

Quiet,
sounds,
creeping
round,
don't,
sound,
only
hum,
Boom!
drum,
fingers
numb,
sound?
Yes,
guess?
Yes,
ghost?
Gulp!
Silent,
hum,
not
fun,
Down!
comes
picture,
of
Mum,
sound?
Yes,
guess?
Yes,
ghost?
Gulp!
Guess
who?
Not
you!

Gone?
Yes,
ghost?
Gulp!

Sophie Cruddas (13)
The Queen Elizabeth Academy, Atherstone

DEPRESSION ...

Depression is like swimming in the Devil's deep pond,
with somebody pulling on you, trying to rip you under.
It's like there is someone or something behind you every corner,
lurking, lingering, hoping you come, hoping they get you this time.
It's like you're being murdered from the inside out,
everyone is blind to it.
Depression is the silent killer, the murderer, the bus to Hell,
it gives you a knife, it tells you to cut, it tells you it's the only exit.
He sits there in the corner; smiling, he's done his job,
he is the thief of minds, the thief of joy, the thief of life.
He seizes your emotions, your soul,
securing his grip, he forces you to hold the rusty knife.
He pushes you to the point of cutting yourself,
he chuckles while the blood trickles down, dripping onto the sink.
It's silent, fleeing, he drops you to the floor,
you cry and shout on the tiles, with no hope,
with no friends, with no joy, with no life.
The life you lived before is just some dried-out memory;
you live in forever sorrow, you never smile.
This is depression.

Eleanor Sleat (13)
The Queen Elizabeth Academy, Atherstone

CRISP, WHITE SNOW

Crisp, white snow,
Gentle to the touch,
Trickling down like icing powder,
Smooth, soft, delightful.
The icy gems, sparkling, glistening,
Quiet, silent on the ground below,
Deep drifts begin to build, reflecting the cold moon's touch,
Glittery, frosty snow,
Like linen sheets just out of the tumble dryer.
By the fire, sizzling hot,
Thoughts of outside, shivering cold,
Like the icy smile of the blood-curdling disguise,
Out in the cold winds,
Howling shrill screeches of glee,
Crunchy steps in the snow,
Everyone treks home with quiet footsteps,
Tucked up, cosy inside,
The ghost of snow's whisper echoes on,
Whilst crisp, white snow pours down once more!

Rachel Jennings (12)
The Queen Elizabeth Academy, Atherstone

MY LITTLE PONY

The pony trots up to me in the field,
swishing her bottom
I enjoy the noise from the pony's hooves
on the floor

When I get on, she bolts,
the horse in the other field frightened her

When I stop her
she begins to buck
Five seconds later, I'm on the floor
with my pony snorting down to me.

Lily Lucy Elizabeth Ledwidge (12)
The Queen Elizabeth Academy, Atherstone

114

MY PET DOG

My pet dog, goes by Storm,
she comes by my side,
she is bluey-grey coloured,
she rolls over for belly rubs.

My dog jumps on the couch cushions,
she doesn't like other dogs,
so when I bring her out for exercise,
she rows with the other ones.

She does growl lots,
you will know if she's in good moods or not,
my dog gets little pots,
in the pots she finds food,
she only gets them when she's in good moods.

Sometimes, she tries to devour my fish,
when she does this I don't put her food in her dish.

My pet dog,
it's the little things that count.

Jack Swann (12)
The Queen Elizabeth Academy, Atherstone

DYING

I lie still, witness the moon climb while the lights glow,
Moist soil douses my lifeless body, soft touch.
Fresh scents fill my nose, it's home.

Humidity confronts me then strikes my cold skin,
I enjoy its feel,
Silence visits me, relieved I won't destroy him,
He brings quilts of serenity.

Feeble gushes of wind rock me,
Telling me I should sleep.

Siân Lewis (13)
The Queen Elizabeth Academy, Atherstone

TICK-TOCK

The clock goes round,
Tick-tock, tick-tock.

The seconds go by,
Tick-tock, tick-tock.

There's one born every minute,
Tick-tock, tick-tock.

Minutes turn into hours,
Tick-tock, tick-tock.

Time is of the essence,
Tick-tock, tick-tock.

When will be your time?
Only you will know,
Tick-tock.

Become one with your destiny,
Your time is slowly ending,
Tick-tock.

Reise Smith (14)
The Queen Elizabeth Academy, Atherstone

THE NIGHT

The night is gloomy, mysterious,
Things hide in the unlit surroundings,
Wildlife thrives through the night,
Owls perch in trees, hooting,
They protect their nests like soldiers protecting their country.

Throughout the night lights will be seen distributed,
They light up the world,
Light removes the dim edge producing light,
The night closes with sunrise.

Alfie Chesters (12)
The Queen Elizabeth Academy, Atherstone

116

MIDNIGHT SKY

Shimmering in the quilt of blue,
my eyes scout for hidden definition,
between the glowing lights.
Turning to see next to me,
the soft, green hills,
with its numerous smiles.
The chill of the night wind,
brushed my thick fleece of skin,
I remember most of the jolly time
while we've been friends.
The music tumbling in the slow breeze
whirls with the colours of the sky.
The moon is out in the twilight,
hidden behind silver clouds.
I lose sight of its profile,
but it's not like the sight
in the never-ending night.

Hannah Walker (13)
The Queen Elizabeth Academy, Atherstone

NEVER-ENDING FRIENDSHIP

Friendship is one of life's stupendous prizes
Friends continue to be trustworthy, will be there to give you hope
They're there to help you
They direct you to move on in life
They will be there for you, non-stop, 24/7
They could be difficult to find or simple
If you find good friends, you will continue to be friends for life
They show your true colours
They give your life cheer
Showering devotion on you
So that your body is full of glee
I love my friends!
Do you love yours?

Courtney Anderson (12)
The Queen Elizabeth Academy, Atherstone

117

SPRING

The morning breeze is crisp,
There is jewel-like dew everywhere,
Covering the ice-frosted ground.

Birds sing their sweet song when the sun rises,
Stirring new life from its cosy sleep,
Young bunnies, sheep, chicks.

Buds on trees,
Blossoming, growing,
Until they're pretty like the rest.

The clocks spring in front by one hour,
Giving us less time in bed during the morning hours,
But the tick-tock of the clock forever goes on.

Spring is the best out of the four,
So get set,
It's soon going to show up.

Emily Jennings (14)
The Queen Elizabeth Academy, Atherstone

THE MOON IS HERE

The wind is blowing in the open
the moon is shining down
everyone feeling emptiness
people wishing for the sun
nothing going right
the people upset
they continue to wish for joy plus cheer

In the morning, kids joking
grown-ups settling, plus enjoying everything
everyone doing fun things
the sun is hot, with hot conditions
but soon the moon will come out
now everyone is returned to be upset.

Liam Carty (13)
The Queen Elizabeth Academy, Atherstone

SOMEBODY LOVES YOU

Exquisite beginnings, broken ends
Forlorn people, mourning one's end.
Your life is like superior gems
Gorgeous, expensive, unique, golden.
Your life is the music sheet
You express feeling through the cuts on your body
Showing you've been strong for too long.
Cold, unloved, broken, wrong
Somebody does love you
You just don't know where they're hiding.
You're not broken, just being strong
Being fixed.
Not cold, either, just waiting
For someone to fire up your soul.
Just remember, someone out there loves you
You just need to find them.

Amelia May Arundel (13)
The Queen Elizabeth Academy, Atherstone

WINTER

The wind whistles violently through the deserted, gloomy streets
Holding icy jewels
They slice through the midnight sky
Dropping quickly, silently onto the frozen ground
While the world is snoring, children sleeping soundly
Thoughts of snow forts, sledges and snowmen filling their youthful minds
When the winter sun begins to climb up through the morning sky
Vehicles start to splutter into life
Children lie in their soft, cosy beds
Snug and drowsy
Suddenly, scurrying outside to explore the white sheet
Covering the countryside
Full of excitement.

James Taylor (13)
The Queen Elizabeth Academy, Atherstone

119

DEPRESSION

Deep in your thoughts,
lonely, depressed,
everyone telling you
you're not the best!

Put down,
you're not worth it,
cyberbullied,
joke,
hypocrite,
don't listen, they told me.

Time to do something,
show them,
It doesn't affect you,
If it doesn't kill you,
you're stronger!

Lillie Hamilton (12)
The Queen Elizabeth Academy, Atherstone

BLUE WINTER

Winter is cold,
like being inside the enclosed freezer.
Winter is not for the wildlife
of the chilled forests.

Winter is blue,
The colour of frosty snow, we know.
Winter is not everybody's type,
due to the slippery world they must trek.

But winter is for me,
I like the snow brick igloos which fit the theme of snow-sphere fights.
Join everyone else
when the blue winter emerges.

Finley Howell (13)
The Queen Elizabeth Academy, Atherstone

DOGS

There's mostly clever ones,
Nobody get concerned,
Turn the other way,
They'll be in your spot,
Completely covered in dog fur.

Been to obedience school,
They know how to mind,
When visitors come round,
They seem to unwind,
Behind in time to their cute polite self.

They produce mess every time,
But they still win,
You, with your friend,
Our times lives too,
We divide with grins.

Alexandru Istrate (12)
The Queen Elizabeth Academy, Atherstone

WINTER

I step outside into the coldness,
I feel the brisk wind brush my skin.
Sheets of clothes, one . . . two . . . three,
but inside the breeze rushes within.

The sky is grey with specks of light,
yet still, the gloom surrounds me.
Pieces of snow plunge from beyond the clouds,
droplets slip through the old spruce tree.

The world is quiet, no sound noted,
neither footsteps nor birds.
Complete silence,
only the whistling of the wind's words.

Evie Findlay (13)
The Queen Elizabeth Academy, Atherstone

WINTER!

Snowdrops glistening in the vivid light,
Covered in white powder,
The most gorgeous sight.
Crisp, soft snow, crunching under your feet.
The scent of firewood burning,
This smell is so sweet.
Gingermen cooking,
Dessert developing,
Children looking,
Nothing could be better.
The cheerfulness building up inside,
Feeling of joy being cried,
Shining sequins up on the tree,
Tinsel, with glitter, lights which glow,
This is where I need to be.

Alexis Perkins (12)
The Queen Elizabeth Academy, Atherstone

XBOX

Xbox is fun
Keeps you out of the sun
On it with your friends
The coolest trend
Committing all the crimes
On it all the time

Xbox is life
Better without the wife
Don't buy PS
Even though it costs less
Keep close to it
Don't move, just sit
Don't lose energy
But use my elegy.

Josh Kirkland (14)
The Queen Elizabeth Academy, Atherstone

SUNSET, SUNRISE

When the stunning, effulgent sun sets,
When the night sky is present,
The world will rest, undisturbed,
Below the moon's soothing crescent.

The wind's loud whisper echoes on,
The wolves begin to howl,
The twigs begin to rustle,
Under the hoot of the snowy owl.

The world is quiet, the world is still,
Set for the sun's next rise,
The world will soon be lit once more,
By tomorrow's sun lighting up the skies.

Eaden Byrne (13)
The Queen Elizabeth Academy, Atherstone

LOVE

Love is the most curious thing,
most desired, most tender of
emotions.

It will be sought forever,
even though it dies,
it's full of empty promise,
trust and dignity,
but forever dies.

Lachlan York (14)
The Queen Elizabeth Academy, Atherstone

EBONY

Ebony is the colour of sorrow, the surround of no joy,
It is like the thing stopping children messing with their toys.
It comes without notice, striking girls and boys,
It could be behind you, composing no noise.

Ebony could kill you at 30 or before,
It comes into your house, ditching the door,
It becomes your room its footsteps heeded on the floor,
It hurts you, exposing gore.

Harry Black (12)
The Queen Elizabeth Academy, Atherstone

THE BIRD'S PREY

The bird,
controlling the sky,
like the queen bees control their hive.
It swoops from side to side,
seeking its prey.
When the bird sees, it strikes,
you will never trick the bird,
or it will have you for its prey.

Charlie Treharne (12)
The Queen Elizabeth Academy, Atherstone

WINTER

The crisp winter breeze,
blows softly in the midnight sky.
The silky, smooth, pure white snow
lying still, on the ground.
Winter, such restful surroundings,
winter, such unique scenery,
winter, you'll know when it's here.

Olivia Burdon (12)
The Queen Elizabeth Academy, Atherstone

THE SWIFT RUNNER

The swift runner is too young,
lost his friend, with him now,
Prince of Troy, shot him here,
with the bow, through the heel,
he is fierce, but gone now,
his girlfriend left lonely,
she will wonder, where is
her swift runner now?

Charles James Townsend (13)
The Queen Elizabeth Academy, Atherstone

FOOTBALL

Like puffs of wind, it gets kicked
on the field
used to be sly for tricks.
Dodging through people
to score in the net.
Guess the score -
no one knows yet!

Chloe Gillett (13)
The Queen Elizabeth Academy, Atherstone

THE UNIVERSE

The universe, the lifeless empty void
which our home is in
full of bright, exciting events
the moon, orbiting close to us.
Mind-blowing moments we wish to see
no one will ever know how big it is.

Ethan Chant (14)
The Queen Elizabeth Academy, Atherstone

SUMMER

Red roses, shine in summer,
smell of freshly cut turf,
blossom on trees looks stunning,
something we never get in the British Isles,
buzzing bees in the hols,
night-time never not messing.

Kurtis Hall (14)
The Queen Elizabeth Academy, Atherstone

Est. 1991

YOUNG WRITERS INFORMATION

We hope you have enjoyed reading this book – and that you will continue to in the coming years.

If you're a young writer who enjoys reading and creative writing, or the parent of an enthusiastic poet or story writer, do visit our website www.youngwriters.co.uk. Here you will find free competitions, workshops and games, as well as recommended reads, a poetry glossary and our blog.

If you would like to order further copies of this book, or any of our other titles give us a call or visit **www.youngwriters.co.uk**.

Young Writers
Remus House
Coltsfoot Drive
Peterborough
PE2 9BF

(01733) 890066
info@youngwriters.co.uk